Reviving the American Dream

Reviving the

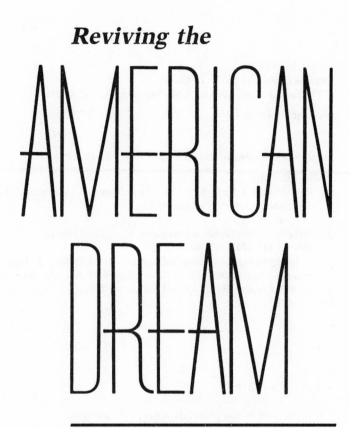

AMERICAN DREAM

The Economy, the States
& the Federal Government

Alice M. Rivlin

THE BROOKINGS INSTITUTION
Washington, D.C.

Copyright © 1992 by
THE BROOKINGS INSTITUTION
1775 Massachusetts Avenue, N.W., Washington, D.C. 20036

LIBRARY OF CONGRESS CATALOGING-IN-PUBLICATION DATA:

Rivlin, Alice M.
  Reviving the American dream : the economy, the states, and the
  federal government / Alice Rivlin.
    p. cm.
  Includes bibliographical references (p.   ) and index.
  ISBN 0-8157-7476-1 (cloth)
    1. Intergovernmental fiscal relations—United States. 2. Federal
government—United States. 3. United States—Economic policy—1981–
4. Industrial productivity—United States. I. Title.
HJ3258.A2R57   1992
33673—dc20   92-16631
                                                       CIP

9 8 7 6 5 4 3 2 1

The paper used in this publication meets the minimum
requirements of the American National Standard for
Information Sciences–Permanence of Paper for Printed
Library Materials, ANSI Z39.48-1984.

⟨B⟩ THE BROOKINGS INSTITUTION

The Brookings Institution is an independent organization devoted to nonpartisan research, education, and publication in economics, government, foreign policy, and the
social sciences generally. Its principal purposes are to aid in the development of sound
public policies and to promote public understanding of issues of national importance.

The Institution was founded on December 8, 1927, to merge the activities of the
Institute for Government Research, founded in 1916, the Institute of Economics,
founded in 1922, and the Robert Brookings Graduate School of Economics and Government, founded in 1924.

The Board of Trustees is responsible for the general administration of the Institution,
while the immediate direction of the policies, program, and staff is vested in the President,
assisted by an advisory committee of the officers and staff. The by-laws of the Institution
state: "It is the function of the Trustees to make possible the conduct of scientific
research, and publication, under the most favorable conditions, and to safeguard the
independence of the research staff in the pursuit of their studies and in the publication
of the results of such studies. It is not a part of their function to determine, control, or
influence the conduct of particular investigations or the conclusions reached."

The President bears final responsibility for the decision to publish a manuscript as
a Brookings book. In reaching his judgment on the competence, accuracy, and objec-
tivity of each study, the President is advised by the director of the appropriate research
program and weighs the views of a panel of expert outside readers who report to him
in confidence on the quality of the work. Publication of a work signifies that it is
deemed a competent treatment worthy of public consideration but does not imply
endorsement of conclusions or recommendations.

The Institution maintains its position of neutrality on issues of public policy in
order to safeguard the intellectual freedom of the staff. Hence interpretations or
conclusions in Brookings publications should be understood to be solely those of the
authors and should not be attributed to the Institution, to its trustees, officers, or other
staff members, or to the organizations that support its research.

Foreword

In recent years, Americans have been increasingly concerned about a double challenge: revitalizing their economy and making their government work better. The economy has been performing poorly for nearly two decades, and the long-run outlook is discouraging. Moreover, the political system appears unable to take decisive actions, such as eliminating the federal deficit and improving education, that would brighten prospects for the economy.

In this book, Alice M. Rivlin examines the two challenges simultaneously and suggests that a key to meeting both of them may lie in restructuring the American federal system. She proposes a cleaner division of responsibilities between the state and federal governments in hopes of improving economic policy and revitalizing government at both levels.

Alice M. Rivlin is a senior fellow in the Brookings Economic

Studies program. She is a former director of that program and was the first director of the Congressional Budget Office. Currently on leave from Brookings, she is a professor of public policy at George Mason University.

Helpful comments on the manuscript were provided by Henry J. Aaron, Gary T. Burtless, Timothy J. Conlan, Edward M. Gramlich, Arthur M. Hauptman, Paul C. Light, Thomas E. Mann, Rudolph G. Penner, Charles L. Schultze, Carol Cox Wait, Joshua M. Wiener, Clifford M. Winston, Sidney G. Winter, Steven A. Wolfe, and an anonymous reader. The manuscript benefited greatly from research assistance by Elizabeth Braeman, Lisa D. Cook, Karen Y. Gee, and Nien-he Hsieh. Valerie M. Owens provided valuable assistance throughout the project, and David J. Rossetti was extremely helpful in preparing the manuscript for publication. Susan L. Woollen prepared the manuscript for typesetting, June R. Smith provided computer assistance, and Gordon Brumm prepared the index. The author also wishes to thank Nancy D. Davidson for expert editing and Roshna M. Kapadia for verifying factual accuracy.

The Brookings Institution is grateful to the Pew Charitable Trusts for a generous grant in support of this project. Chapter 2 also draws on Alice M. Rivlin, David C. Jones, and Edward C. Meyer, *Beyond Alliances: Global Security through Focused Partnerships*, a study funded by the John D. and Catherine T. MacArthur Foundation and the Rockefeller Foundation.

BRUCE K. MAC LAURY
President

May 1992
Washington, D.C.

Contents

1. The Dream, the Reality, and Some Solutions   1

  A Time for Rethinking

  Three Personal Biases

  The Growing Consensus on Economic Policy

  The Case for Rethinking Federalism

  Proposals for the Future

2. Federal Policy Goes Global   20

  New Dimensions of National Security

  America Faces Up to Globalization

  Implications for the Job of Governing

3. Long-Term Goals for the Economy   32
    Getting Beyond the Short Run
    Defining a Successful Economy

4. Good News and Disappointment   42
    The Good News Years
    The Disappointing Years

5. What Went Wrong and What to Do about It   65
    The Productivity Mystery
    The Mystery of Rising Inequality
    The Saving Mystery
    The Medical Cost Mystery
    The National Dilemma

6. The Evolution of American Federalism   82
    Changing Views of Federalism
    Small Government and Dual Federalism
    Two Reasons for Federal Growth
    Building National Institutions
    Influencing and Reforming the States
    The States Rise to the Challenge
    Mandates
    Whither Federalism?

7. Rethinking Federalism   110
    Three Scenarios
    The Rationale for "Dividing the Job"
    *Two Previous Attempts to Sort Out
    Responsibilities*
    How "Dividing the Job" Differs

8. Paying for Stronger States   126
    Where the Money Comes From
    State and Local Fiscal Stress

Unequal State Resources
Interstate Competition
Casualties of Go-It-Alone Taxation
Common Shared Taxes: A New Approach
Making the Decisions
The German Approach to Fiscal Federalism
The Politics of Common Shared Taxes

9. Social Insurance: A Federal Priority 153
The Case for Social Insurance
Reforming Health Insurance
Strengthening Social Security

10. Federalism Faces New Challenges 177
The Economic Challenge
The Institutional Challenge
Improving the Policy Process

Recommended Readings 183

Index 188

ONE   *The Dream, the Reality,*
           and Some Solutions

The "American dream" may sound vague
and grandiose, but it means something concrete and important
to many Americans. It means an economy in which people who
work hard can get ahead and each new generation lives better
than the last one. The "American dream" also means a democratic political system in which most people feel they can affect
public decisions and elect officials who will speak for them.

In recent years, the dream has been fading. Americans are
worried about their economic future—and they should be. For
nearly two decades, the much-vaunted American economy has
been performing below par. Wage earners have found their take-
home pay buying less. Families have kept up their standard of
living by working more hours and having both spouses in the
labor force. Young people look at their job prospects and wonder
whether they will do as well as their parents or will be able to

own a house. Parents worry about their children's future. Many children face bleak futures: one in five now lives in poverty.

Pocketbook worries are compounded by fear that the quality of American life is deteriorating. Violence is pervasive; city streets and parks are unsafe; drug addiction is epidemic; racial tensions are high. Toxic wastes, dirty air, and traffic gridlock increase the hazards and reduce the enjoyment of daily living, especially in densely populated areas.

The American democratic system, although admired around the world, is not confronting the public problems that concern its citizens most. The federal government can lead an international coalition to victory in the Middle East, but appears far less decisive at home. The budget deficit has paralyzed policy for more than a decade. Neither major political party has a convincing domestic agenda; neither can articulate a clear view of what the federal government ought to do. State and local governments are more sure of their roles, but most are being forced to cut their activities in the face of serious financial crises.

The tone of domestic political discourse is as worrisome as its substance. Candidates impugn each other rather than proposing solutions. People elected to lead and govern point fingers at each other: the president blames Congress, and Congress blames the president. Politicians pay more attention to interest groups than to the public interest. Average citizens feel no one cares about them. Allegations of mismanagement and corruption fill the press. Cynics about government find much to be cynical about.

A TIME FOR RETHINKING

It is time for Americans to ask themselves: What is wrong and what can we do about it? Why is an economy with such rich natural resources and such a vigorous, talented population not performing better? How can we get it back on track? Why is such an experienced democratic government so paralyzed? What can we do to make the political system work better? This book is an invitation to the reader to think about these questions and to explore some possible answers.

You do not need a Ph.D. to read this book. It is intended for anyone interested in public issues and worried about the future of the country, not just for "experts." Big decisions about economic policy and government activity should not be left to experts. Unless substantial numbers of citizens make the effort to get into the discussion—to think and talk and argue about what kind of economy they want and what they and their elected leaders should do—the country will not function well. Unfortunately, public policy experts, including my fellow economists, often do more to obscure than to illuminate the issues that deserve public discussion. They focus on technical details rather than basics. They argue about weapons systems rather than the reasons for needing and using military force or about obscure provisions of the tax code rather than how to pay for public services. They talk to each other in mumbo jumbo on talk shows and at conferences, while the public tunes out.

The fault is not just with the way experts talk about public policy, but also with policy itself. Laws, regulations, and the processes by which they are made have become unproductively complex. There are so many centers of power, overlapping jurisdictions, and complicated procedures that it is hard for both participants and onlookers to figure out who is in charge of what and whom to blame when things go wrong. The process of making decisions on the federal budget, for example, has become so byzantine that even members of Congress find it incomprehensible. The press and the public are totally mystified.

Incomprehensible policies and procedures breed cynicism and distrust of government. Citizens who are mystified often suspect something nefarious is going on behind closed doors. Taxpayers who have no clear idea what their money is buying resent having to pay the bill. Hence every effort to make government work better must include the instructions: simplify, clarify, demystify. This book focuses particular attention on one aspect of those efforts: sharpening the distinction between federal responsibilities and those of state and local government.

THREE PERSONAL BIASES

All authors have their biases. One of mine is optimism. I believe that America's current economic and political problems

are serious but not insurmountable, and that we will find ways
to solve them.

Many recent books about the future of the United States
predict either imminent catastrophe—a terrible crash or deep
depression—or the country's slow decline into the status of a
third-rate power. Some are pulp sensationalism, written for people who enjoy wallowing in gloom and doom. Others are by
serious scholars. One of the best is by Professor Paul Krugman
of the Massachusetts Institute of Technology.[1] Krugman points
to most of the same economic problems highlighted here and
suggests many of the same solutions, but he does not expect
corrective action. He predicts that Americans will simply accept
stagnating standards of living, increasing disparities between
rich and poor, growing indebtedness to the rest of the world, and
a slow decline of the country's international status.

Krugman may be right, of course, but the pessimistic out-
comes he expects are preventable. Americans have always been
ingenious, creative, and hardworking; the U.S. economy has far
greater resources than most others. The challenges it confronts
pale beside those facing the crumbling economies of the former
Soviet bloc. I do not believe we will be so shortsighted or irresponsible as to wander unnecessarily into terminal decay.

My second bias is pragmatism. I am a fanatical, card-car-
rying middle-of-the-roader. The recommendations of this book
cannot easily be classified as either liberal or conservative, and
its message will not appeal to ideological purists of either the
left or the right. The recommendations reflect both a strong belief
in the efficacy of private markets and a conviction that public
action is often necessary and constructive. Those who believe
that private enterprise is always more efficient or that government activity always serves the public interest—regardless of
the circumstances—are giving away an important set of tools for
making society work better.

My third bias is against magic wands and painless solutions.
Everyone looks for ways of accomplishing ambitious goals without effort—lose weight without dieting, learn French while you
sleep. Extreme versions of "supply-side economics," popularized

1. Paul Krugman, *The Age of Diminished Expectations: U.S. Economic
Policy in the 1990s* (MIT Press, 1990).

in the 1980 presidential campaign, promised Americans that cutting taxes would invigorate the economy so much that government revenues would rise and deficits would disappear. It sounded too good to be true, and it was.

If simple, painless solutions to public problems existed, they would have been found long ago. Significant public objectives—eliminating the federal deficit, reducing poverty and pollution, raising productivity—cannot be attained without effort and conflicts. Some of the conflicts are among groups of people—rich and poor, old and young, rural and urban. These conflicts are agonizing because more for one group often means less for another. Painful compromises must be worked out. Even more difficult conflicts arise among values, often those held by the same people. Most Americans, for example, would like to help people in genuine need, especially children. At the same time, they would like to encourage self-reliance and hard work. It is not easy to design policies that do both. Resolving these conflicts and hammering out solutions require patience, effort, flexibility, and a willingness to sacrifice for the common good.

The performance of the economy and the functioning of the political system are usually discussed by different people in separate books. One set of authors diagnoses the ills of the economy and offers economic policy prescriptions; another set focuses on the failings of politics or politicians and recommends reforms in the political process. Both sets of authors often act as though the federal government were the only government that mattered and all new public policies ought to be made in Washington.

This book attempts to bring economic and political issues together and to reexamine the roles of federal and state governments. It raises three sets of questions.

—What policies are needed to brighten the economic future of Americans?

—Why is our political system not functioning to put these policies into effect?

—What could be done to improve the functioning of both the political system and the economy?

It offers a package of recommendations designed to fit together and reenforce each other.

THE GROWING CONSENSUS ON ECONOMIC POLICY

Surprisingly, there is not much controversy raging over what to do to improve America's economic prospects. In fact, a broad consensus has emerged in recent years—among liberals and conservatives, business groups, workers, and citizen organizations—on the need to accomplish one fundamental objective: raising American productivity. To live better in the future, Americans need the skills, the tools, and the organization to work more effectively at whatever they do, whether it is making cars, teaching children, or building houses. The agenda for increasing productivity growth, in turn, boils down to an instruction worthy of Ben Franklin: save and invest, invest and save. To revitalize the American economy, we must modernize factories, offices and equipment, transportation, and communications. We must stay on the forefront of science and technology and make sure that new investments improve rather than degrade the environment. Above all, we must enhance the knowledge, skills, vitality, and creativity of the present and future work force. If America is to have a bright future, we must invest in our young people, especially those likely to have the least skills and opportunities.

Much of the needed investment—physical, human, and intellectual—should be undertaken by private enterprises, new and old, large and small. However, there is growing agreement—even, or perhaps especially, in the business community—that private investment is not enough. Private entities alone cannot improve the effectiveness of schools and training, rebuild roads and bridges and airports, support basic science, reduce crime, and improve the quality of air and water and the livability of American communities. Community commitment and public action at all levels of government are required.

The resources needed for investment in future productivity growth have to come from somewhere. Americans will either have to consume less of their current income and save more, or they will have to use the savings of foreigners. In the last decade, American saving has plummeted and American investment has been increasingly financed by foreign capital. Investment by foreigners is a lot better than no investment at all: it creates productive jobs for American workers. Reliance on foreign capital is precarious, however, and it has an inevitable consequence:

foreigners end up owning a lot of American stocks and bonds, factories, hotels, and office buildings. The profits, interest, and dividends from these assets flow to other countries, not to the United States.

Hence, if Americans want to enjoy the benefits of their own higher productivity, they will have to increase their own national saving. As I shall show in chapter 5, an effective way to increase national saving is to reduce the government's borrowing; in other words, reduce the federal budget deficit. If the government were borrowing less, even running a surplus, more resources would be available for private investment to increase future productivity. Therefore elimination of the federal budget deficit would make a crucial contribution to income growth.

Consensus is also growing that America's system of paying for health care is out of control and needs an overhaul. Skyrocketing health care costs, amounting to more than 13 percent of GNP in 1991, are an increasing burden on individuals, businesses, and government. At the same time, a large fraction of the population is without adequate health insurance coverage. More and more groups are calling for a new health financing system that will both ensure basic coverage for everyone and slow the increase in costs.

Although there is disagreement about the details, almost everyone who writes and speaks about the revitalization of the American economy comes up with the same list of policy imperatives: increase public and private investment, especially in technology, skills, and infrastructure; get rid of the federal deficit; and reform the health payment system to cover more people and slow cost growth. The big question is not what needs to done, but why so little is happening and how to get more action.

There are many theories about why our public institutions are so paralyzed and how to get them moving again. This book turns the spotlight on one explanation: confusion between the federal government and the states over who should be in charge of what. Its central theme is that both federal and state governments would function better—and the policies needed to energize the economy could be carried out more effectively—if a cleaner distinction were made between the responsibilities of the federal government and those of the states. The federal government and the states should divide the public tasks needed to get the economy functioning well. In particular, (1) the federal government should control the growth of health care costs and ensure that everyone has health insurance coverage; (2) the federal government should move from deficit to surplus in its budget; (3) states should take primary responsibility for a productivity agenda involving education, work force skills, and public infrastructure, while the federal government should retreat from these areas; and (4) a new system of common shared taxes (explained below) should be adopted to help put state financing on a more secure and less unequal footing.

THE CASE FOR RETHINKING FEDERALISM

The argument about which functions should be exercised by the federal government and which by the states has been going on for more than two hundred years. There are no "right" answers. The prevailing view shifts with changing perceptions of the needs of the country and the relative competence and responsiveness of the states and the federal government.

Until the 1930s, the federal government had limited powers and spent relatively little money except in time of war.[2] Government services were not as extensive as they are now, and most were performed by states and their localities. In this period of "dual federalism," the powers of the federal government and the states were viewed as separate and distinct, not overlapping. Then, over the half century between 1930 and 1980, Americans laid increasing responsibilities on the central government. All levels of government grew, but the power, functions, and budget of the federal government grew most rapidly.

Americans turned to Washington for two distinct sets of reasons. First, the collapse of the economy in the Great Depression convinced many people of the need for national institutions to strengthen the economy and deal with problems that states could not be expected to handle on their own. The federal government created social security, set up the unemployment insurance system, developed river basins to control flooding and produce

2. For a somewhat more detailed history of the shifting roles of state and federal government, see chapter 6.

power, supported agricultural prices, strengthened banking and credit systems, and began regulating many economic activities.

Second, activists and reformers turned to Washington, especially in the 1960s, out of frustration with the way states and localities were performing their traditional functions. Compared with the federal government, states had limited capacities and resources. Their staffs were unsophisticated and unprofessional. Their legislatures, dominated by rural members, were unresponsive to city dwellers and minorities. Many state governments were overtly racist. Hence the federal government enacted a range of programs designed to influence the level and nature of state spending in areas that had traditionally been states' responsibilities, such as education, job training, health services, waste treatment, and housing. Many federal grants bypassed states entirely and went directly to local governments, especially big cities.

The surge of federal activities had many positive results, but it also diffused accountability and directed the energies of reformers toward Washington. Citizens concerned about improving state and local services began joining national organizations to lobby for federal money, rather than working at the state or local level. States and localities, even universities, established Washington offices, hired consultants, and acquired expertise in federal grantsmanship.

The proliferation of federal programs, projects, offices, and agencies in so many parts of the country made the federal government increasingly unmanageable. It resembled a giant conglomerate that has acquired too many different kinds of businesses and cannot coordinate its own activities or manage them all effectively from central headquarters.

Then the reaction set in. The flood of federal funds for state and local government crested in the late 1970s and ebbed in the 1980s. Tax cuts and defense spending increases created a huge federal budget deficit that precluded new federal domestic activities. States and cities had to rely more on their own resources. Moreover, the perception of superior federal competence, which had propelled Washington into many traditionally state areas, faded. Reforms gave states stronger governors, more representative legislatures, and more professional and sophisticated civil servants. Meanwhile, the federal government lost some of its former luster. The savings and loan debacle and scandals in defense procurement and housing programs undermined the presumption that the federal government managed more effectively than the states. The intertwining of state and local responsibilities and the diffusion of accountability remained, however.

In the 1990s the United States faces an urgent need to revitalize its economy and to get its political system off dead center and functioning responsively again. There are at least four reasons to think that reraising the fundamental questions of federalism—which level of government should do what and where the revenues should come from—would help in meeting these challenges.

The Impact of Global Interdependence

The first reason is that dramatic changes in the world are radically altering the tasks facing national governments. Rapid advances in the technology of transportation, communications, and weaponry have shrunk distances and intertwined the United States with the rest of the world, intimately and irreversibly. Goods, services, money, and people are flowing easily across oceans and borders. So are economic, political, and environmental problems.

Global interdependence requires international cooperation to solve common problems and some delegation of sovereignty to supranational authorities. The Gulf war and growing nuclear capacity in developing nations leave no doubt that stronger international controls are needed on sophisticated weapons. The rapidly thinning ozone layer dramatizes the stake that all nations have in controlling harmful atmospheric emissions.

Despite its political appeal, isolationism is no longer a viable option. If the United States is to protect its own citizens and help shape a more habitable world, it must take an active part in international partnerships focused on everything from chemical weapons to acid rain to narcotics traffic. These partnerships are already demanding increasing attention from both the executive and legislative branches of the federal government.

Global interdependence creates a paradox for the U.S. government. On the one hand, since both the president and Congress will be spending greater time and energy on international affairs, domestic policy will get less attention in Washington. At the same time, global interdependence makes domestic policy more important than ever. The United States needs rising productivity, a skilled labor force, and modern physical capital, both public and private, if it is to generate the improved standard of living necessary not only to foster domestic well-being, but also to play an effective role in international partnerships. The added complexity of Washington's international role strengthens the case for sorting out domestic responsibilities more clearly. Washington cannot do everything and should not try. The states should take responsibility for a larger and more clearly defined segment of the domestic agenda.

Top-down and Bottom-up Reform

A second and more important reason for rethinking the division of responsibilities is that some of the policies needed to revitalize the American economy require bottom-up community effort that cannot be imposed from the top down. They require experimentation and adaptation to local and regional conditions, and that can come only from the state and local level, not from Washington.

Improving education will take bottom-up reform. Presidential speeches and photo opportunities, national testing and assessment, federally funded experimental schools, even new grants spent in accordance with federal guidelines, can make only marginal contributions to fixing the schools. Education in America will not improve significantly until states and communities decide they want better schools. Making education more effective will take parents who care, committed teachers, community support, and accountable school officials. An "education president" can help focus media attention on schooling, but he risks diluting state and local responsibility by implying that Washington can actually produce change.

The popular federal Head Start program demonstrates that preschool education helps children from poor families cope better in school. The negative legacy of Head Start, however, is that states and communities have come to believe that the responsibility for preschool education lies with Washington, not with them. Change would come more rapidly if concerned citizens, parents, and educators worked to improve their own preschools instead of lobbying Washington to allocate more funds for Head Start.

Street crime, drug use, and teenage pregnancy are all examples of problems that the federal government can deplore but cannot fix. A resurgence of community concern and effort is needed. Social services, housing, community development, and most infrastructure also must be carefully adapted to the needs of particular places. Federal grants can help defray the costs, but at the price of confusing the issue of who is responsible and who needs to take action.

On the other hand, there are important public functions that Washington performs well and state and local governments cannot address effectively. First, there are inherently central responsibilities, like national defense and foreign affairs, for which the federal government must represent and defend the interests of the country as a whole. Second, there are activities whose benefits clearly spill over state lines—such as air traffic control, basic scientific research, and prevention of river pollution or acid rain. Individual states have little incentive to undertake these programs because so much of the benefit would go to people in other states. Third, there are programs whose workability depends on having a uniform national system, such as social security.

Social security is perhaps the federal government's greatest domestic success. It is well administered and immensely popular. People are less resentful of social security taxes than other taxes, because they know what the money goes for and they expect benefits themselves. Because it involves tracking people over a lifetime, social security could not easily be handled by the states; too many people would move in and out of state systems and end up with conflicting and overlapping coverage.

The federal government is also best adapted to solving the double problem of controlling rapidly rising health costs and providing health insurance to the whole population. The U.S. health care system is the most expensive in the world, now consuming more than one-eighth of everything the nation produces, but it does not provide commensurate benefits. Millions of people are left out or inadequately insured. State-by-state efforts to expand insurance coverage and control medical costs are not likely to be successful. Sentiment is growing for some kind of national health insurance system that would provide universal coverage for basic health services and would control costs by setting reimbursement rates for doctors, hospitals, and other medical providers.

Another important role that the federal government is uniquely positioned to play at the moment is increasing national saving. Americans are saving by contributing to social security. The social security system is currently running significant annual surpluses because taxes collected exceed benefits paid out. These reserves will be needed to pay benefits to the large baby boom generation when its members retire. They ought to be used to help finance the productive investment needed to generate higher incomes in the future. At present, however, the social security surpluses are simply being lent to the rest of the government to offset part of the huge federal budget deficit. For the savings of working Americans to be used productively, the federal deficit must be eliminated (see chapter 5).

The Need for More Tax Revenue

The third reason for focusing on the assignment of tasks to federal and state governments is that all levels of government are in serious financial difficulties. Even if some services are cut back and others are run more efficiently, more revenues are needed to eliminate deficits at the federal, state, and local levels, to accomplish the productivity agenda, and to reform health care financing. If taxes must go up, it is important to consider which level of government will make best use of the revenues.

The federal fiscal crisis. The federal budget deficit is the biggest single impediment to revitalizing the American economy. It diverts a large portion of America's inadequate supply of saving into financing the ongoing expenses of the government rather than productivity-enhancing investment. It puts upward pressure on interest rates and requires that a substantial share of federal tax revenues be devoted to debt service. It has paralyzed the federal government's ability to address new problems, at home and abroad, and weakened its ability to combat recession.

Despite more than a decade of efforts to reduce it, the

federal deficit is definitely not withering away. To be sure, the recession and the savings and loan bailout combined to increase the deficit in 1991 and 1992 to levels that are not likely to continue. Even without these temporary upward pressures, however, the Congressional Budget Office (CBO) projects that the federal deficit will still be above $200 billion in 1996. Moreover, the CBO expects the deficit to rise significantly by the beginning of the next century if policies are not changed.[3] Why would CBO expect the deficit to rise if tax and spending laws do not change? A big part of the answer is that the costs of medicare and medicaid are projected to keep going up faster than revenues if nothing is done to control medical care prices.

The unfortunate fact is that if the federal government retains its present portfolio of responsibilities (even with declining defense spending), it cannot balance the budget, much less get to surplus, *without raising taxes.* Even bigger tax hikes will be required if the federal government is to take on new responsibilities. The only option for eliminating the deficit without a significant federal revenue increase would be to count on the states for the productivity agenda and also to devolve big chunks of current federal responsibilities to the states. This would move the financing crisis from the federal to the state level.

The state fiscal crisis. Increasing the responsibilities of state and local governments is a dubious proposition because they too are in fiscal trouble. At first glance, their fiscal distress seems more temporary than that of the federal government. State and local governments generally suffer serious fiscal stress in recessions. Their revenues fall off as sales, income, and property values stop growing or decline while claims on their services continue to increase. Because, unlike the federal government, states and localities cannot normally borrow to cover operating expenses, they are forced to raise taxes and cut services as soon as their reserves are exhausted.

Even after the economy returns to moderate growth, however, there are reasons for pessimism about the prospects for state and local finance in the 1990s. The fiscal health of state

3. Congressional Budget Office, *The Economic and Budget Outlook: Fiscal Years 1993–1997* (January 1992), p. 30.

and local governments declined in the second half of the 1980s. Pressures for spending outran revenues. The fiscal stress, especially in cities, reflected the growth in crime, drug addiction, AIDS, homelessness, and poverty, all of which continued to increase through the long recovery from the recession of the early 1980s. Moreover, a major villain of the federal budget drama appears again at the state and local level. Rising medical care costs, especially for medicaid, have put enormous pressure on state and local budgets that seems unlikely to abate.

Thus all levels of government will probably face continuing fiscal stress in the 1990s. Policies to revitalize the economy—increased public investment, a federal surplus, health financing reform—cannot be undertaken without more revenue at some level of government. The public seems angry and dissatisfied with government, however, and unwilling either to increase its support or to accept a lower level of services.

Dissatisfaction with Government

The fourth reason for questioning the jobs assigned to various levels of government in the 1990s is the American public's dissatisfaction with politics and politicians. Many Americans have "tuned out" political debate and stopped participating in elections. Polls reveal declining confidence in political leaders, rising skepticism that public officials care about the views of ordinary people, disgust at political campaigns, and cynicism about the democratic process.

There are many possible reasons for the disparagement of government: the need to blame someone for the stresses of a faltering economy, the influence of big money on political campaigns, the negativism of political advertising, and the insensitivity of politicians to the damage done to their collective image by even minor peccadillos such as getting parking tickets fixed. Some blame the ideological polarization of the major parties—the capture of the Republicans by ultraconservatives and the Democrats by extreme liberals—for leaving the pragmatic, middle-of-the-road majority without leadership.[4] Others point to the

4. E. J. Dionne, Jr., *Why Americans Hate Politics* (Simon and Schuster, 1991).

widening gulf between elites, who see public policy as a matter of technical control, and a general public that correctly perceives the elites' contempt for citizens' opinions.[5]

The blurring of state and federal roles contributes to cynicism about politics. For example, much of the rhetoric in the 1988 presidential campaign concerned issues over which presidents have little control—crime, drugs, education, child care, and industrial development. Voters care about these issues, but they also know that Washington is too remote from them to make a difference. Candidates for federal office undermine their credibility by implying these problems have national solutions and by refusing to address serious federal issues, such as the budget deficit.

Voters also appear more willing to pay taxes if they know that revenues will be used for identifiable services important to them. Polls show voters opposed to paying more taxes for undisclosed purposes but willing to pay for improved schools or increased environmental protection. In recent years the federal government's general revenues (other than social security and medicare payroll taxes) have declined as a percentage of GNP, while state and local revenues have increased substantially. Perhaps taxpayers are clearer about their need for state and local services and are more willing to pay for them than for the more remote services of the federal government. Despite substantial increases in payroll taxes for social security and medicare in recent decades, polls show these taxes are less unpopular than the federal income tax, presumably because taxpayers know what the payroll taxes buy and value the benefits. Hence the most feasible way to increase revenue may be to earmark new taxes for a particular federal benefit such as health insurance or for improved services at the state and local level.

PROPOSALS FOR THE FUTURE

This focus on federalism suggests several quite drastic proposals aimed at reenergizing the American economy and restoring confidence in the political system. Their basic theme is that

5. Daniel Yankelovich, *Coming to Public Judgment: Making Democracy Work in a Complex World* (Syracuse University Press, 1991).

the federal and state governments should divide the jobs to be done and get moving.

—*The productivity agenda*. The states should take charge of the primary public investment needed to increase productivity and raise incomes, especially to improve education and skill training and modernize infrastructure.

—*Devolution*. The federal government should eliminate most of its programs in education, housing, highways, social services, economic development, and job training.

—*Common shared taxes*. With federal blessing, or even the assistance of the federal government, states should strengthen their revenue systems by cooperating in collecting common taxes to be shared among them on a formula basis.

—*Health care financing*. The federal government should adopt a plan that will ensure basic health insurance coverage for everyone and control the increase in health costs.

—*Federal budget surplus*. The federal government should run a surplus in its whole budget (counting social security), thus reducing federal debt service costs and adding to the pool of saving available to finance private investment.

These proposals fit together. State responsibility for the productivity agenda would sharpen the distinction between federal and state tasks, making it easier for citizens to understand what each level of government does and to blame the right set of officials for poor performance. Devolution would take whole areas of public spending out of the federal budget, making it easier to move that budget toward surplus. More important, making clear that the devolved functions belong to the states, not the federal government, would transfer pressure for increased spending in these areas from Washington to state capitals and help keep federal deficits from recurring.

The resulting fiscal pressure on states and localities would be alleviated in two ways. First, federal responsibility for health care financing, coupled with strong cost controls, would relieve states and localities of the escalating burden of medicaid and reduce the cost of other public medical care. Second, the adoption of one or more common shared taxes would improve the states' collective revenue-raising capacity.

One example of a common shared tax would be a uniform

state sales tax (or value-added tax) collected at the same rate on the same items and shared on the basis of population. A uniform corporation income tax, collected along with the federal income tax and shared on a formula basis, would make tax compliance simpler for multistate corporations. A common state energy tax could reduce pollution and promote conservation as well as raising revenue (see chapter 8).

The idea of states sharing common taxes is a radical departure from the American tradition that each state must go it alone in levying taxes. In other federal systems, tax sharing is more usual. In Germany, for example, the central government collects most of the taxes and shares the proceeds with the *Länder* (states). German taxpayers, individual and corporate, fill out only one income tax return, for both federal and state taxes. German firms pay a value-added tax whose proceeds are shared between the federal government and the states, with disproportionate shares going to the least affluent states to help equalize services.

As the American economy becomes more national and international, the case for more coordination of state taxation increases. People, companies, sales, and services move with greater ease across borders. One consequence is that states and localities have to worry about keeping their tax rates from getting out of line with those of other jurisdictions. Another is that more and more companies, and even individuals, owe taxes in multiple jurisdictions. The resulting complexity is costly for both taxpayers and tax collectors.

Like federal grants, common shared taxes could be designed to improve the relative position of the least affluent states. Unlike federal grants, however, they would not cause confusion about which level of government has responsibility for particular programs or impose federal rules and guidelines on state and local authorities.

To revive the American dream, citizens must find new energy and commitment to revitalize the myriad institutions that influence American life—families, businesses, schools, unions, churches, clubs, and government at all levels. They must be willing to experiment, restructure, and try new approaches to old and new problems. In the words of David Osborne and Ted Gaebler, they must even "reinvent government" by breaking out of old hierarchical patterns and empowering those closest to the problems to participate in finding solutions.[6]

A first step is to reexamine that peculiarly American institution, federalism. The current confusion of responsibilities between federal and state government is undermining confidence in government and impeding the implementation of policies needed to restore a healthy economy. Sorting out the roles more clearly could break the logjam, help both levels function more effectively, and improve both domestic and foreign policy.

6. David Osborne and Ted Gaebler, *Reinventing Government: How the Entrepreneurial Spirit Is Transforming the Public Sector* (Addison-Wesley, 1992).

TWO   *Federal Policy*
            Goes Global

In the last few decades, the explosive advance of technology has eroded distance to the point of insignificance. Ballistic missiles cross oceans in minutes; financial transactions leap continents in seconds. Television brings desert war into American family rooms, along with famine in Africa, assassination in India, and confrontation in Moscow and Beijing. Radio reports the Nikkei average and the Dow Jones, the price of gold in London and of pork bellies in Chicago. Muscovites line up at McDonald's; Nebraskans drive Hyundais. People worry about environmental hazards, not just from local waste dumps, but from the burning of tropical forests, oil spills, or nuclear explosions in distant parts of the globe. Whether they like it or not—and many do not—Americans find themselves intimately and continuously entangled with the rest of the world.

The shrinking of the world is not reversible. We have to learn to live with it. It requires fresh thinking about the structure of our government and the division of responsibilities in our federal system.

NEW DIMENSIONS OF NATIONAL SECURITY

Protecting America's national security is arguably the federal government's most important job. The increasing interdependence of the world, however, profoundly changes the nature of national security and complicates the task of protecting it. Until recently, the security of nations was mostly a matter of military power. As the world has become more interdependent, security has taken on more economic, environmental, and political dimensions.

Moreover, in an interdependent world, no nation can guarantee its own security. Cooperation is necessary. Treaties, mutual agreements, and rules of international behavior have to be worked out and enforced—to reduce the danger of nuclear war, avoid environmental destruction, halt the speed of contagious disease, keep trade flowing, or prevent financial collapse.

The Military Dimension

The advent of nuclear weapons, and missiles to deliver them with almost no warning to all parts of the globe, profoundly altered the military dimension of security by making "winning" an all-out war impossible. Nuclear weapons threatened the survival not only of the combatants, but of neutral nations and possibly of the human race itself. In less than a century, threats to military security had moved from local to regional to global. Security was no longer ensured by either attacking or defending, but rather by preventing the use of weapons of mass destruction.

The collapse of the Soviet empire makes war among the major powers unlikely. Now the greatest military threat to global security is the proliferation of sophisticated weapons in the developing world. Iraq's invasion of Kuwait dramatized the fact that a growing number of countries with simmering antagonisms and potentially irresponsible governments have acquired highly sophisticated weapons. Some have nuclear and chemical weapons and the means to deliver them and more are likely to

FIGURE 2-1. *U.S. Exports and Imports, 1950–90*

Percent of GNP

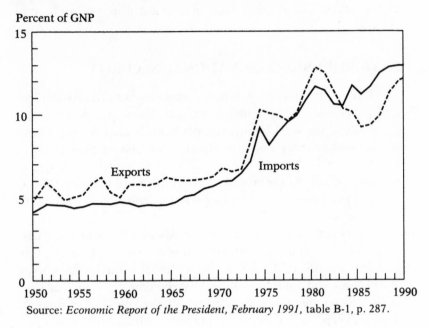

Source: *Economic Report of the President, February 1991*, table B-1, p. 287.

have them in the future. The addition of India in 1989 to the list of countries that have successfully tested medium-range ballistic missiles illustrates that lethal technological capabilities are not confined to high-income countries. The number of countries able to threaten world security is rising rapidly. Unless the major nations cooperate to halt weapons proliferation, deter and punish aggression, and encourage peaceful resolution of disputes, the consequences for all could be dire.

The Economic Dimension

Since the end of World War II, trade among nations has grown substantially faster than domestic output. As may be seen in figure 2-1, both the imports and the exports of the United States roughly tripled as a percentage of GNP between 1950 and 1990.

Because it is so large and has such diverse resources, the United States remains more self-sufficient than most industrial economies. Germany and Japan, and especially small economies like Sweden and the Netherlands, are far more dependent on exports and imports than the United States is. Nevertheless, Americans are gradually coming to realize how crucial international trade has become to the daily functioning of their economy. American willingness to go to war to defend Kuwait from Iraq's aggression clearly demonstrated the importance of imported oil. Foreign-made consumer goods are seen now not as luxuries, but as items used daily. Television sets, videocassette recorders, and stereo systems are predominantly imported or composed of foreign-made components. Even the military is significantly dependent on weapons and other materials imported from abroad. At the same time, a widening variety of American businesses are marketing a growing share of their products and services overseas. Big exporters include grain farmers, producers of computer hardware and software, aircraft manufacturers, movie makers, heavy construction companies, and purveyors of accounting and consulting services. The spending of foreign tourists bolsters the U.S. travel, hotel, and recreation industries. American colleges and universities derive a significant portion of their revenue from educating foreign students.

The globalization of finance has been even more dramatic than the growth of trade. Between 1973 and 1989, foreign bank deposits in industrial countries rose more than twice as fast as total deposits. Foreign exchange transactions in New York increased more than sevenfold between 1980 and 1989, while at least equal growth occurred in the London and Tokyo markets.[1] Worldwide computer and other communications networks now link financial markets in all parts of the globe instantaneously. U.S. companies that never used to borrow abroad now routinely borrow from foreign banks and market their securities wherever it is most advantageous. These increased movements of capital across borders have greatly reduced the differences in the cost of capital among countries. National markets for money and securities have been merged into a single global capital market.

---

1. Twentieth Century Fund, *Partners in Prosperity: The Report of the Twentieth Century Fund Task Force on the International Coordination of National Economic Policies* (New York: Priority Press, 1991), p. 4.

Most of the effects of financial globalization are positive. Investment projects that promise a good rate of return can be financed quickly and for about the same cost almost anywhere. Jobs and income are created in the process. The downside is that negative economic events are also transmitted rapidly around the world. A fall in the Japanese stock market can send prices on Wall Street plummeting. A country defaulting on its debt or the collapse of a key bank could weaken the whole international financial structure and threaten the solvency of banks and financial institutions around the world. Central bankers in all major countries communicate constantly and worry about the health of each other's banking systems almost as much as they worry about their own. The collapse of the Bank of Credit and Commerce International (BCCI) in 1991 illustrates the problems posed by institutions operating in international financial markets in secrecy and without adequate regulation.

The health of the American economy depends increasingly on the prosperity of its trading partners and on the smooth flow of trade and finance across borders. Preventing calamity and making sure that American interests are protected requires that the federal government work with other countries continuously to make sure trade rules are fair and enforced, the financial system is solid, and Americans are not hoodwinked by unscrupulous financiers operating under less rigorous rules than our own. In addition, as their economies become more and more intimately intertwined, countries will find it more necessary to coordinate tax policies and major economic decisions whose effects spill across borders.

The Environmental Dimension

Until quite recently, foul air, polluted water, or depleted soil were local problems affecting jobs and health in the immediate area. Now the world is beginning to realize how easily environmental destruction moves across borders.

Direct threats to human health and life, including improper disposal of chemical and nuclear wastes, can bring death, disease, and discomfort to people far from the source of the problem. The accident at the Chernobyl nuclear power plant spewed deadly fallout across international borders. A chemical spill in one country can be carried rapidly downriver to others. The sulfur and nitrogen oxides emitted by coal-burning power plants fall as acid rain in distant places and damage forests, fish, and human health. Release into the atmosphere of chlorofluorocarbons and halons, two types of chemicals used extensively in industry, depletes the ozone layer and permits increased penetration of the lower atmosphere by ultraviolet radiation. The increased radiation, in turn, causes a greater incidence of skin cancer and cataracts and interferes with the human immune system.

The world has also become uncomfortably aware that continued emission of greenhouse gases into the atmosphere is likely to raise global temperatures. Although the effects of such warming on global and regional climate are uncertain, the worst-case possibilities are alarming. Changes in precipitation patterns could turn the U.S. wheat belt into a dust bowl. Ocean currents could shift, possibly altering regional climates drastically. Melting polar ice and thermal expansion of the oceans could raise the sea level significantly. Because the effects of global warming are likely to be irreversible by the time they become evident, it is only prudent for the nations of the world to cooperate to control greenhouse gas emissions.

The Political Dimension

Modern communications, especially the worldwide availability of television, have made people in distant places conscious of each other's standard of living and social and political rights. The poor and oppressed know that it is possible to live better lives, to have more material possessions and more control over their destiny. People in more affluent and freer societies are more conscious of poverty and assaults on human rights in other parts of the world: witness the number of Americans concerned about apartheid in South Africa, suppression of freedom in China, or hunger in Ethiopia. This interlinking of world communication means that local and regional conflicts can escalate rapidly to matters of global concern.

AMERICA FACES UP TO GLOBALIZATION

The world has been growing more interconnected and interdependent for a long time. The implications of this for U.S. policy and the daily business of government, however, are only slowly dawning on Americans, in part because the confrontation with the Soviet Union dominated policy attention for so long.

At the end of World War II, the United States and its allies were intensely conscious of the interdependence of the world and the need for international institutions to keep the peace and promote trade and development. They launched the United Nations with the hope that it would evolve into a strong international structure for resolving disputes and keeping peace. The United States also played a lead role in establishing and financing the International Monetary Fund, the World Bank, and the specialized organizations of the United Nations dealing with food and agriculture, children, refugees, health, trade, development, and other matters of urgent international concern.

The Cold War: An Expensive Interruption

The confrontation between the United States and the Soviet Union derailed the post–World War II optimism about global cooperation. It split the world into two hostile camps and reduced the United Nations to an acrimonious international debating society. America's view of its own role shifted from builder of worldwide institutions to leader of the anticommunist coalition. Containment of the Soviets became the basic—almost the only—theme of U.S. foreign policy.

For forty years, the size, structure, and location of U.S. military forces, both strategic and conventional, were determined by their primary mission: to deter Soviet attack on the United States and its allies and to defeat Soviet forces if deterrence failed. The developing world was seen as divided into Soviet client states and those of the "Free World," and American policies were designed to hold countries in the U.S. camp. Trade policies penalized communist countries' exports and prevented them from importing goods that might enhance their military capability. Cultural exchanges, tourism, sports events, and immigration policy all became weapons in the cold war confrontation.

The dramatic events in Eastern Europe and the Soviet Union that followed the opening of the Berlin wall in 1989 began by shattering the image of the Soviet Union as a menacing superpower bent on world domination and ended by shattering the

Soviet Union itself. Their economies in shambles, the republics of the former Soviet Union are struggling with the horrendous task of preventing chaos while moving to a more productive market system.

National Security in the 1990s

The end of the confrontation with the Soviet Union creates two related opportunities for the United States. The first is to take a new and more realistic look at the problems that beset the world and what role the United States can and should play in resolving them. The second is to redeploy as effectively as possible the considerable resources that are no longer needed to deter or counter Soviet aggression. These resources include not only steel and coal, oil and food, and fibers and plastics, but the effort and talents of scientists, engineers, and many other people at all skill levels in both the public and private sectors.

The basic question is what will replace containment of the Soviet Union as the organizing principle of America's stance toward the world. Many are tempted to replace an old enemy with a new one—to identify Japan as the nation to beat in an economic power struggle or to make Iraq into a prototype of potential foes in the developing world.

The threat-response mindset of the past, however, seems inappropriate to dealing with the challenge of enhancing security in the twenty-first century. Many of these challenges are not traceable to a malevolent enemy who can be identified, destroyed, or contained. Nuclear fallout could come from negligence or an isolated act of sabotage in an obscure nuclear power plant. A round of protectionist actions and reactions, in which each nation tries to shelter its own industries, could reduce the standard of living for everyone. Actions of ordinary individuals trying to make a living around the world—clearing forests, catching fish, using fuel, making industrial products—can cause irreversible damage to the planet's land, air, and water.

Most of the challenges to U.S. security in the post–cold war world cannot be met by the United States alone, but require cooperative international effort. Nations must work together to control weapons, reduce the pressure of population on resources, prevent irreversible damage to the environment, settle disputes without resorting to war, maintain stable trade and financial networks, assure increasing viability of the economies of developing nations, and facilitate the successful transition of planned economies to market systems.

Many of these challenges, especially in the developing world, are interrelated and reinforce each other. Poverty and population growth exacerbate deforestation, soil erosion, and depletion of other resources, as is evident in much of Africa and vast regions of Asia and Latin America. The result can be starvation and streams of economic and environmental refugees moving into cities and surging across borders in search of food and work. Economic tensions polarize groups and aggravate national, ethnic, religious, and ideological tensions. Conflicts resulting from these tensions are increasingly unlikely to remain local. Mass communications make the whole world witness to the conflict. The wide availability of high-technology weapons makes any conflict more dangerous, not only to the combatants but to their neighbors and the rest of the world.

Eventually a global federal structure may be necessary to resolve conflicts that threaten world security. For the foreseeable future, however, international cooperation will be far more feasible if it addresses specific problems on an ad hoc basis. This will require U.S. involvement in an overlapping network of international partnerships focused on issues as disparate as controlling chemical weapons and enforcing copyright law. Encouraging these problem-solving partnerships and helping them succeed should replace containment of communism as the dominant objective of American foreign policy.

The fact that the United States no longer dominates the world economy as it did at the end of World War II can be viewed as an advantage in foreign policy. As long as the U.S. economy is healthy and the standard of living is growing, the fact that Europe, Japan, and the emerging industrial nations are also prospering is a plus for the United States. This collective prosperity means these nations can share the economic and political costs of ensuring peace, revitalizing Eastern European economies, fostering third world development, and reducing environmental degradation.

However, the diffusion of economic power requires the

United States to change its leadership style. Multinational cooperation will become more mandatory than optional. We will have to lead actively, offering cooperative solutions to world problems and negotiating, implementing, honoring, and helping to enforce them. In an era when the United States can no longer dominate economically, leading by persuasion, example, and coalition building becomes increasingly important.

IMPLICATIONS FOR THE JOB OF GOVERNING

In the new interconnected world, the job of protecting national security is bigger and more complicated than ever before. All branches of the federal government are devoting increasing time and effort to matters that involve other countries and international organizations. International affairs have become the daily preoccupation, not just of professional diplomats, but of officials with a wide range of responsibilities. The president and his staff deal with more countries and more international organizations on more issues than would have been thought possible a generation ago.

Moreover, national security and international affairs are less shrouded in secrecy and less dominated by technical experts than before. At the height of the cold war, most Americans, even most people who follow public policy issues, felt ill equipped to evaluate the Soviet threat and the appropriateness of responses to it. They felt that because the consequences of Soviet attack were so overwhelming and the knowledge required to assess the risks was dependent on secret intelligence, they had no real choice but to accept whatever the national security experts said. Moreover, the national security establishment did nothing to encourage open debate on alternative strategies and often suggested that those who questioned policy, especially the need for additional weapons spending, were disloyal or soft-headed. Even in Congress, basic issues of national security strategy were rarely debated.

In the post–cold war world, however, there are as yet no experts. The issues are more diverse and less dependent on secret information. Individuals and their legislative representatives feel less intimidated by national security professionals. The congressional debate in January 1991 over whether to launch an attack on Iraq, for example, was an unusually thoughtful and forthright airing of alternative views on the merits of military action versus continued reliance on economic sanctions.

Members of Congress are more knowledgeable and concerned about international issues than ever before. A growing number of congressional committees deal with foreign matters. Although congressional involvement in foreign policy is often resisted by the White House and professional diplomats, who still regard foreign policy as their exclusive domain, congressional concern reflects public concern. Now that interrelations with other countries affect average Americans so directly, Congress must make international matters an increasingly important part of its job. The executive branch will have to get used to sharing power, as it always has in domestic matters.

President George Bush and other federal officials have been criticized for paying too much attention to foreign affairs. Given the importance of the rest of the world to America's future, they cannot responsibly reduce their concern with international matters, although they will have to do a better job of explaining their preoccupation to the voting public.

The inexorably rising frequency and complexity of U.S. interaction with the rest of the world add to the stress on federal decisionmaking processes and underline the need for making those processes simpler and more effective. If the United States is to be an effective world leader, it cannot afford a cumbersome national government, overlapping responsibilities between the federal government and the states, and confusion over which level is in charge of specific domestic government functions.

As the world shrinks, international concerns will continue threatening to crowd out domestic policy on the federal agenda. Paradoxically, however, effective domestic policy is now more crucial than ever, precisely because it is essential to U.S. leadership in world affairs. Unless we have a strong productive economy, a healthy, well-educated population, and a responsive democratic government, we will not be among the major shapers of the future of this interdependent world. If the American standard of living is falling behind that of other countries and its governmental structure is paralyzed, the United States will find its credibility in world councils eroding. International considerations provide additional rationale, if more were needed, for the United States to have a strong effective domestic policy.

One answer to this paradox is to rediscover the strengths of our federal system, the division of labor between the states and the national government. Washington not only has too much to do, it has taken on domestic responsibilities that would be handled better by the states. Revitalizing the economy may depend on restoring a cleaner division of responsibility between the states and the national government.

THREE   *Long-Term Goals*
for the Economy

What should Americans expect from their economy? How should they assess whether it is performing well or badly? Most questions about the health of the economy relate to the short-run ups and downs of the business cycle. If the economy is recovering from recession, people are generally optimistic. They are likely to return incumbent politicians to office. If unemployment is rising, or prices are soaring, people are gloomier and readier for a political change.

Preoccupation with the immediate, however, obscures the longer-term trends that determine how the economy will be performing in the future and whether the next generation will live better than this one. This chapter asks what aspirations Americans should have for their economy over two or three decades. It suggests an answer: if the economy is performing well, it should generate sustainable and widely shared growth in the standard of living. Meeting this test is crucial not only to the domestic economy, but also to a healthy political system and to America's capacity for international leadership.

GETTING BEYOND THE SHORT RUN

When most people think of the state of the economy, they focus on what is happening right now or what is likely to happen in the next few months. News reports both reflect and reinforce this interest in the immediate.

Media Economics

The media report a new economic statistic almost every day: last quarter's gross national product, last month's unemployment rate, last week's automobile sales, yesterday's stock market index, today's gold price. A glutton for current economic statistics has a large menu to choose from.

The press treats the economy like a patient with mysterious ailments whose temperature, pulse, and respiration need continuous monitoring. Economists are cast as the medical team, updating reports on the patient's vital signs and giving short-run prognoses. An economist who appears on a talk show is asked: When will the recession end? Is inflation accelerating? Will interest rates go up? Will the value of the dollar fall in international markets? And, of course, what will happen to the stock market?

Actually, most economists, like doctors, are reluctant to make predictions, and those who make them are seldom accurate. The economy, like the human body, is a highly complex system whose workings are not thoroughly understood. Moreover, the short-run movements of the economy are strongly influenced by unpredictable noneconomic events, such as election results, wars, or natural disasters. The only thing forecasters can do is examine the relationships among past measures of economic activity and use those relationships to guess what will happen next. Some do this by constructing elaborate computer models of the interaction of economic forces in the past; others make less formal projections based on hunch, experience, and calculations on the back of the proverbial envelope. All are subject to error, because the economy and the forces that affect it— including public policies—are in a constant state of change.

The barrage of statistics on the economy spews forth from

the media with so little context or explanation that it seems designed to confuse, not enlighten. Indeed, television presents statistics more comprehensibly when it deals with the weather than when it deals with the economy. A good weather telecast shows high- and low-pressure areas, cold fronts, cloud cover, and storm systems developing at a distance and moving toward the area in question. The viewer ends up, not just with a forecast of the day's weather, but with a reasonable sense of the interplay of meteorological forces that affect the weather and the degree of uncertainty that attaches to the forecast. The consumer of economic news is not so fortunate.

Nevertheless, people grasp for indicators of the economy's current health and listen avidly to predictions of imminent change, even when they know such predictions are often unreliable. This is not surprising since the short-run ups and downs of the economy can drastically affect individuals, families, and businesses. When economic activity slows or declines, many people suffer and many more worry that they will. In a recession, sales fall, workers lose jobs, construction declines, profits plummet, and businesses fail. Recovery brings happier news—rehirings, more sales, higher profits, and greater survival chances for new and old businesses. The downside is that high levels of activity—or a sharp increase in an important price, such as oil—can set off inflation, which erodes savings and hurts lenders and people on fixed incomes.

Underlying Trends

The obsession with the business cycle is not surprising, but it ignores underlying trends that have a more permanent effect on how well people live. On the average, families lose ground in a recession and make it up in the recovery. If the average income is rising significantly over the longer run, the downturns will be easier to bear and the average family will be substantially better off after a decade or two. If the average rise in incomes is 2 percent a year, the typical family will be nearly 50 percent better off in twenty years; if it is 3 percent, they will be more than 80 percent better off. If incomes rise only half a percent a year, the average family will live less than 11 percent better after twenty years. Moreover, if the distribution of income is becoming less equal—the gap between rich and poor is widening—then a substantial number of people will be worse off after a few years, even if the average income is rising, and especially if it is rising slowly.

After the recession of 1980–82, the economy experienced a long slow recovery lasting well into 1990. The fact that no recession occurred for seven years made many people feel that the economy was performing well. The length of the recovery eclipsed the facts that the average standard of living had barely risen at all since the early 1970s, that inequality in the distribution of income was growing, and that many people were, in fact, worse off.

Underlying trends are crucial. Fortunately, economists are on far more solid ground in analyzing the long-run trends and their consequences than they are in predicting next week's stock prices.

DEFINING A SUCCESSFUL ECONOMY

There is no obvious single measure of how well the economy is performing in the long run, and there is lots of room for argument about what aspects are important and how to measure them. At a minimum, Americans ought to want three things from their economy: the average standard of living should be rising; the improving level of living should be shared by all groups; and the rising standard should be sustainable. All three elements of this definition are important.

A Rising Standard of Living

In an economy that is performing well, average people live better than their parents did and can expect that their children will live better still. This expectation of improvement has always been an important part of the American dream.

Unfortunately, changes in the average standard of living are not easy to measure precisely, especially over substantial periods of time. One rough measure is per capita national income—the value of everything the nation produces in a year, minus an allowance for the physical capital used in producing it, divided by the size of the population.

Per capita income is not a perfect measure of what is happening to the average standard of living. For one thing, it does not include anything that is not sold for a price, such as services people produce for themselves at home or for others as volunteers. Moreover, improvements in the quality of products and services are not adequately reflected in per capita income. For example, astonishing changes in human well-being brought by modern sanitation and medical advances, such as antibiotics, have occurred over the last century. The fact that few modern parents experience the pain of losing a child to the infectious diseases that used to kill so many children is not captured in comparisons of per capita income. Nor is the convenience of having an automatic teller machine on the corner. On the other hand, deterioration in the quality of life, caused by air and water pollution or traffic congestion, for example, is not captured either. Hence national per capita income is at best a rough approximation of the standard of living.

Moreover, rising income or purchasing power seems a disturbingly materialistic goal, especially for a society in which the average family is already as well fed, clothed, and housed as the average American is today. Should we be setting our sights on the acquisition of more and more possessions? For their own good, should not most Americans be eating fewer calories rather than more, exercising rather than acquiring a second or third car, and concentrating on the moral and spiritual side of life rather than on the accumulation of additional objects? These questions are well worth pondering, but it should be remembered that a rising income allows people to buy more education, recreation, and travel, more medical care, closer communications, more skilled personal and professional services, and better-designed as well as more numerous products. It also means more art, music, poetry, theater, and drama. It can even mean more time and resources devoted to spiritual growth and human development.

A generally improving standard of living generates hopes and confidence and reduces the number of people who feel they are failing. Not everyone will do well, of course. But if the average standard of living is rising, most people will live significantly better than their parents did. Young people who grew up in deprived circumstances will have more chances to prosper.

A rising standard of living makes many choices less agonizing and contentious. A family whose income is rising does not always have to give up something when a new need arises. A society with increasing resources can afford both greater private well-being and improved public services. As incomes rise, constant tax rates generate higher revenues. It is possible to have better schools, roads, and other public services without actually raising tax rates. (Although, of course, demands for public services may still outrun the available public resources.) A society with rising income can assist the less fortunate without forcing the more fortunate to accept cuts in their income.

To be sure, just as money does not always buy happiness for individuals or families, rising incomes do not always lead to harmonious politics. Public choices remain difficult and contentious, even in affluent countries. One reason may be that rich countries, like rich people, have a huge set of choices about what goods and services to provide and how to pay for them, including options to borrow now and pay later. Poor countries have fewer options. They have to defend their borders and provide basic services. They have a hard time obtaining credit from international lenders. Moreover, according to one theory, rising incomes intensify political struggles because they escalate the competition for goods that are physically scarce (such as seashore property) or socially scarce (such as political power or access to the "best" universities).[1]

Nevertheless, just as most people prefer more income to less, most would rather live in a society in which average incomes are rising, winners outnumber losers, and new initiatives do not have to be paid for by reducing some ongoing activity, public or private.

As discussed in chapter 2, the world of the future will be increasingly interlinked as well as potentially dangerous and unstable. Growing threats to international security—political, economic, or environmental—can be reduced only by effective international cooperation and problem solving. If the United States is to be a leader of international partnerships to reduce

1. Fred Hirsch, *Social Limits to Growth* (Harvard University Press, 1976).

threats to its own and the world's security, it must have a vigorous economy with rising average income.

We must be able to contribute our share to the cost of
peacekeeping forces, international efforts to reduce environmental damage, multinational scientific research, disaster relief, and
aid to developing economies. The resources required could be
substantial, especially with respect to the environment. If the
advanced industrial countries are to secure the cooperation of
much poorer countries in preserving the ozone layer, controlling
hazardous wastes, and preventing irreversible damage to land,
atmosphere, and oceans, they are going to have to set a good
example and foot a substantial share of the bill. A stagnant U.S.
economy would likely mean an American public unwilling to
contribute to joint international efforts. Failure of the United
States to contribute, in turn, would greatly reduce the chances
of successful solutions to international problems.

Moreover, if the American standard of living were to fall
progressively behind that of Japan, Europe, and other industrial
countries, we would gradually, but definitively, lose the respect
of the rest of the world and our capacity to lead would be weakened. We do not need the highest standard of living in the world
to command international attention, but we could not avoid
losing influence if the U.S. standard of living were to fall significantly behind that of other major industrial countries.

All Groups Sharing

Increases in the average standard of living do not indicate
satisfactory economic performance if those increases are confined to the favored few or even the favored many. A rising
average does not constitute success if substantial groups of people are being left out and falling further behind the rest of the
population. The situation is especially worrisome if the people
being left out of the general prosperity are clearly identifiable
both to themselves and to others because of race, sex, ethnic
origin, or some other visible characteristic. If those who lose out
are disproportionately concentrated in identifiable groups, they
are bound to feel resentment and to allege favoritism and discrimination. Moreover, separation of the disadvantaged groups
from the rest of the society is likely to be self-reinforcing. If people

with specific characteristics are perceived as less successful, this fact is likely to undermine their confidence, discourage them from investing in education, and perpetuate stereotypes that lead to both increased discrimination and further lack of success.

Broad sharing of prosperity in America, like average rising income and sustainability, has international as well as domestic importance. U.S. efforts to encourage other countries to assist their poor and minorities and to promote freer market systems are undermined if the U.S. market system is visibly failing identifiable groups at home.

Sustainability

Individuals often increase their immediate standard of living in ways that reduce it later—by piling up credit card debts that have to be repaid out of future income, for example. Nations can be shortsighted too, so it is important to make certain that increases in the national standard of living are not achieved by creating serious problems for the future.

Economic growth accompanied by high inflation, for example, is neither desirable nor sustainable. Inflation distorts the economy. It encourages people to put their money in real estate and art objects rather than in investments that enhance future productivity. It favors debtors over creditors and discourages savers.

Nations, like individuals, can borrow beyond their capacity to repay, default on obligations, and damage their creditworthiness. They can borrow to finance consumption or ill-conceived investments and end up with burdensome interest charges and repayment obligations that reduce their future standard of living.

Economic activity that fails to replace the capital it uses is also unsustainable. Accounting principles that apply to companies require recognition that capital assets wear out and must be replaced. However, public capital such as roads, bridges, schools, and government buildings is often allowed to wear out or fall into disrepair without people recognizing that the future national standard of living will be reduced by such shortsighted policies. The decay is often gradual and the cost spread widely. Deteriorating roads, for example, cause accidents, delays, excess fuel consumption, and repair bills paid by owners of cars and trucks, not the government. For taxpayers and vehicle users together, building a highway to a high standard of durability and keeping it in repair can be much less costly in the long run than building it cheaply and repairing it sooner.[2]

Economic growth can also be unsustainable if it damages the environment in ways that lower the standard of living in the future. Shortsighted agricultural development in vast areas of the United States in the nineteenth and early twentieth centuries depleted the soil and created the dust bowl. Deforestation in the Himalayas is producing fuel shortages, soil erosion, and flooding that threaten the livelihood of people in wide areas. The burning of tropical forests in the Amazon basin exposes poor soil that cannot support farming or ranching for long periods, as well as contributing to the buildup of greenhouse gases and destroying the treasures of the forests themselves. Development that pollutes lakes, rivers, and oceans or leads to buildup of toxic waste or mountains of trash and garbage cannot be sustained for long.

Most of the attention to sustainability and economic development in recent years has been focused on the environment and on less developed countries. Where people live at the margin of subsistence, there is great potential for famine and other disasters as a result of shortsighted practices. Moreover, the loss of millions of species from rapid destruction of tropical rain forests, extinction of wild animals in Africa, and the squandering of other irreplaceable assets of developing countries has aroused concern around the world for the common heritage of the planet.

Taking a longer view of economic processes, however, is no less important to the developed countries. Life in the United States could be far less attractive, healthy, and safe if economic growth destroys the natural beauty of the country, poisons the atmosphere, and pollutes the lakes and streams. Moreover, the United States cannot be effective in convincing developing countries to reform their practices if it fails to adhere to sustainable policies itself. American credibility in urging conservation of tropical forests is greatly undermined by our own rapid destruc-

2. Kenneth A. Small, Clifford Winston, and Carol A. Evans, *Road Work: A New Highway Pricing and Investment Policy* (Brookings, 1989), chap. 1.

tion of the ancient forests of the Pacific Northwest. Similarly, it is hard to preach responsible fiscal policy to developing countries when the United States is running huge deficits in its federal budget.

The next chapter looks at the actual performance of the American economy over the last half century. To what extent has it produced sustainable and broadly shared increases in the standard of living?

FOUR   *Good News and*
Disappointment

F

or more than three decades—from the be-
ginning of World War II through about 1973—the United States
was enormously successful in almost every economic dimension. During these "good news" years the average standard
of living rose steeply. Disparities narrowed between rich and
poor, black and white. Americans were saving, investing,
and building for the future. Only a few concerns—about mounting environmental hazards or the deterioration of central cities,
for example—raised any doubts that success could be sustained.

Then disappointment set in. Average Americans were still
living better than people in most other countries, but their incomes were no longer rising much. Progress against poverty
ceased, and the gap between rich and poor widened. In the 1980s
the well-off prospered, but the income of those in the lower

brackets dropped—not just relatively, but absolutely. Short-sightedly, Americans were building up debts, becoming dependent on foreign capital, allowing the nation's infrastructure to deteriorate, and failing to acquire the skills needed for a productive modern economy.

THE GOOD NEWS YEARS

World War II, for all its horrors and destruction, ushered in an extraordinary period of prosperity for Americans. The war ended the Great Depression of the 1930s. It brought jobs to idle workers and orders to underutilized factories, required rapid modernization of production, caused an explosion of scientific advances and technological applications, and opened opportunities for millions of people to move into skilled and well-paid jobs. Families who had scraped through the grim days of the Great Depression suddenly found themselves with money in the bank.

At the war's end, many economists expected another serious depression. They were wrong. America's industries had been energized and modernized by the war effort. There was a huge pent-up demand for consumer products and housing at home. There were vast potential markets for American goods and technology in war-ravaged countries that were now struggling, with American help, to rebuild their economies. The U.S. economy was poised for three decades of rising prosperity. The strong upswing was interrupted by occasional recessions, but all proved short and shallow by comparison with the Great Depression of the 1930s.

An Improving Standard of Living

As a result of high birthrates in the postwar years, combined with declining death rates and substantial immigration, the U.S. population rose by 60 percent between 1940 and 1973. The total output of the economy—the gross national product in constant prices—soared 255 percent in the same period.[1] This surge in the nation's per capita production of goods and services made it possible for almost everyone to live better and for the nation to improve both its public and its private capital at the same time.

1. *Economic Report of the President, February 1990*, pp. 294, 329.

FIGURE 4-1. *Median Income of U.S. Families, 1947–90*[a]

Thousands of 1990 dollars

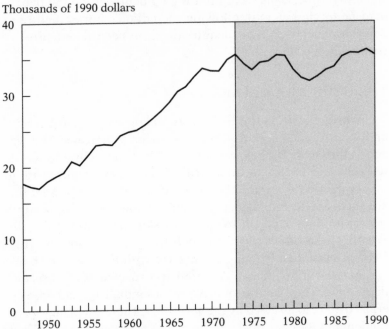

Source: Bureau of the Census, "Money Income of Households, Families, and Persons in the United States: 1990," *Current Population Reports*, series P-60, no. 174 (Department of Commerce, 1991), table B-4.

Most people's standard of living moved steadily upward. The median family's income, adjusted for inflation, grew at an average rate of 2.7 percent a year between 1947 and 1973 (see figure 4-1).

Families had more income primarily because wages were rising faster than inflation in almost every industry and occupation. The wages and salaries of young people went up especially rapidly, in part because young workers had more education than older ones. But older workers also did substantially better economically than the older workers of the preceding generation. The average income of middle-aged men (45–54 years old) who worked full time year-round approximately doubled (allowing for inflation) between 1946 and 1973.[2]

2. Frank Levy, "Incomes, Families, and Living Standards," in Robert E. Litan, Robert Z. Lawrence, and Charles L. Schultze, eds., *American Living Standards: Threats and Challenges* (Brookings, 1988), p. 113.

The rising prosperity had one overriding explanation: the rapidly increasing productivity of American workers. Indeed, there are only two ways in which the standard of living of a population *can* rise. One is that people do more work, either because a higher proportion of the population is employed or because workers put in more hours. The other is that workers produce more per hour worked. In other words, their productivity increases.

Except at the beginning of World War II, the rising incomes of the good news period did not reflect higher proportions of people at work. The fraction of the population that was employed declined somewhat between the end of World War II and the mid-1960s, both because the proportion of children grew so rapidly and because the growth of social security and private pensions enabled older Americans to retire earlier. Then employment began to rise again as the baby boom generation (and their mothers) joined the labor force (figure 4-2).

Incomes rose steeply in this period because productivity growth was rapid. Output per hour worked rose more than 3 percent a year in 1948–65. The increase slowed to just over 2 percent a year for 1965–73—still an impressive rate of growth.[3] This astonishing increase in output reflected improved technology, modernization of factories and offices, increasing education of the labor force, and movement of workers from farms to manufacturing.

Broad Sharing of the Gains

The prosperity of the good news period was shared by the fortunate and the less fortunate. Between 1947 and 1973, families near the middle of the income distribution had the most rapid income gains. Incomes of those at the bottom and the top of the income distribution grew almost as fast (figure 4-3).

The distribution of income in the United States has always been far from equal. In 1949, for example, the one-fifth of American families with the lowest incomes received 4.5 percent of total family income while the top fifth received almost ten times as much. By 1974, the distribution of income among families had

3. Martin Neil Baily and Alok K. Chakrabarti, *Innovation and the Productivity Crisis* (Brookings, 1988), p. 3.

FIGURE 4-2.   *Employment as a Percentage of Population, 1940–90*[a]

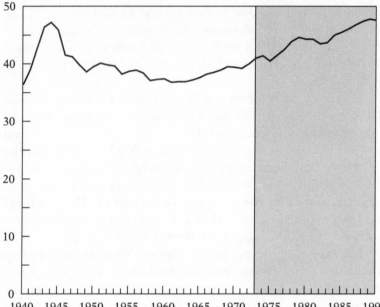

Source: *Economic Report of the President, February 1991*, table B-32.
a. Before 1950, includes civilian labor force for people aged 14 and over; from 1950–90, includes those aged 16 and over.

become slightly less unequal. The share of the bottom fifth had risen to 5.5 percent—still a small fraction, but a perceptible increase—while that of the top fifth had fallen slightly.[4] Although the movement toward greater equality was small, almost everyone felt significantly better off because incomes were rising so rapidly at all levels.

The Decline of Poverty

In the Great Depression of the 1930s, millions of workers lost their jobs as the unemployment rate reached 25 percent of

4. Bureau of the Census, "Money Income of Households, Families, and Persons in the United States," *Current Population Reports*, series P-60, no. 162 (Department of Commerce, 1988), p. 42; and *Current Population Reports*, series P-60, no. 174 (Department of Commerce, 1991), p. 202.

FIGURE 4-3.   *Annual Rate of Change in Family Income in Selected Percentiles of Distribution, Selected Periods, 1947–90*

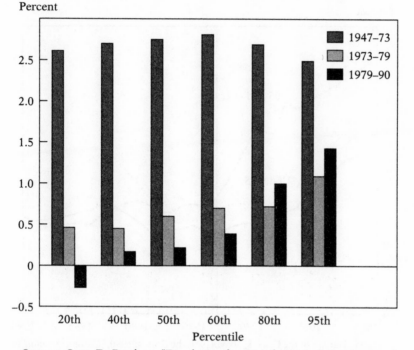

Percent

Legend:
- 1947–73
- 1973–79
- 1979–90

Percentile: 20th, 40th, 50th, 60th, 80th, 95th

Source: Gary T. Burtless, "Trends in the Distribution of Earnings and Family Income: Effects of the Current Recession," testimony before the Senate Committee on the Budget, February 22, 1991, fig. 3.

the labor force. Hunger and malnutrition were widespread. A large fraction of the population lacked adequate food, shelter, clothing, and medical care. There was no official definition of poverty, but when President Franklin D. Roosevelt spoke of "a third of a nation ill-housed, ill-clad, ill-fed," he reflected the scale of the destitution by the standards of the time.

In the 1940s and 1950s, the proportion of people in economic distress dropped rapidly, although depressed rural areas and urban slums remained. The plight of those left out of the general prosperity went largely unnoticed until the 1960s, when America rediscovered the poor and the federal government launched the war on poverty (see chapter 6). One by-product of the war on poverty was the development of an official definition of poverty

FIGURE 4-4. *Poverty Rate for Total Population, Elderly, and Children, 1959–90*

Percent

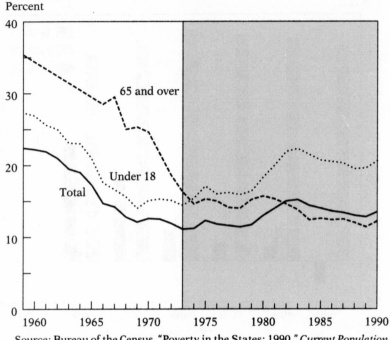

Source: Bureau of the Census, "Poverty in the States: 1990," *Current Population Reports*, series P-60, no. 175 (Department of Commerce, 1991), pp. 16, 18.

based on estimates of the income families of various sizes needed to maintain a minimum decent standard of living. By this definition, about 22 percent of the population had cash incomes below the poverty line in 1959. The poverty rate dropped rapidly to 11 percent by 1973 (figure 4-4).

Thanks mostly to rising social security benefits, the chance of being poor dropped faster for people 65 and over than for the rest of the population (figure 4-4). Public programs also helped the nonelderly poor. A rising proportion of low-income mothers with children received assistance under aid to families with dependent children (AFDC) in the 1960s and early 1970s, for example.

Most of the reduction in poverty among younger people,

however, resulted from high employment levels and rising wages, not from public benefits. Wages for unskilled jobs kept up with those for higher-skilled jobs. As young people obtained more education and older workers with less education retired, there were fewer unskilled workers seeking jobs. Employers had to raise wages in order to hire workers for jobs that required less than a high school education. This narrowing disparity in income between workers with different education levels helped to close the gap between rich and poor, old and young, and blacks and whites.

The position of blacks, starting from a desperately low level, improved dramatically in the good news period. In 1940 most blacks lived in the rural South and had meager incomes. The mechanization of agriculture and the new opportunities in industry during and after the war accelerated the move of the black population to cities and out of the South. The civil rights revolution of the 1960s opened new opportunities. In 1939 the per capita income of blacks was only 39 percent of white income; by 1971, it was 57 percent.[5] The poverty rate dropped rapidly for blacks, although it remained far above the rate for whites. In 1973 blacks were still more than three times as likely as whites to be poor.

A Private and Public Building Boom

In the good news period, the quality and quantity of American housing took a quantum leap. Millions of new houses and apartments were built in the suburbs that sprouted around urban centers. Rising incomes, low interest rates, low down payments, and favorable income tax treatment of home mortgage interest combined to make owning a home possible for an increasing proportion of the population. Along with improved housing came rapid sales of refrigerators, dishwashers, and other consumer durables. The number of automobiles soared as more families bought not just one car, but two or more.

Moving a substantial portion of America to the suburbs required new streets, water and sewer systems, hospitals, and

5. Gerald David Jaynes and Robin M. Williams, Jr., eds., *A Common Destiny: Blacks and American Society* (Washington: National Academy Press, 1989), pp. 271–74.

other public facilities. The babies born in the postwar years poured into the elementary schools, then the junior and senior high schools, and eventually into colleges. Postsecondary education expanded rapidly long before the baby boomers reached college age. Returning soldiers, first from World War II and then from the Korean War, used their veterans' benefits for postsecondary education. More high school graduates went on to college, and many adults also enrolled in higher educational institutions. The most rapid enrollment increases occurred in community colleges. All this education at all levels required buildings.

At the same time, America was modernizing its transportation system. The outpouring of automobiles and trucks required new and wider highways. Increasing use of airplanes required not only airports, but a national system of air traffic control. The interstate highway system, launched in 1956, was the most conspicuous achievement of a public construction boom that included airports, public hospitals, schools, office buildings, and power projects (figure 4-5).

Growth of Government Spending

The public building boom was just a part of the rise in public spending that occurred in the good news period. Public spending at all levels of government—federal, state, and local—increased from 18 percent of GNP in 1947 to 30 percent in 1973 (figure 4-6). Most of the increase in state and local spending was financed out of state and local taxes, but grants from the federal government to states and cities also grew rapidly (see chapter 6).

At the state and local level, spending increases primarily reflected the needs of the younger generation. Public education was a growth industry. At the federal level, by contrast, the needs of older people dominated. Social security outlays grew rapidly as more people became eligible and benefit levels were increased. Medical insurance for the elderly (medicare) was added in 1965. Other types of entitlement programs (in which people with specified characteristics are entitled to benefits) also grew, including veterans' benefits and, especially in the 1960s and 1970s, assistance to low-income people. Total federal payments to individuals rose from about 4 percent of GNP in 1947 to more than 8

FIGURE 4-5. *Public Nonmilitary Construction, 1947–90*[a]

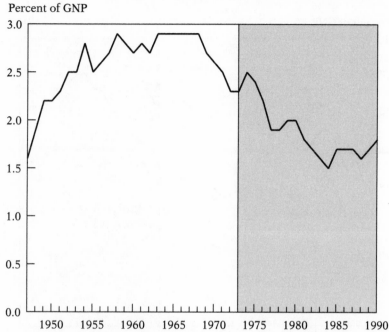

Source: For 1947–85, U.S. Department of Commerce, Bureau of Economic Analysis, *Fixed Reproducible Tangible Wealth in the United States, 1925–85* (June 1987), table B-13; for 1986–90, U.S. Department of Commerce, Bureau of Economic Analysis.

a. Includes buildings (industrial, education, hospital, general office, police and fire stations, courthouses, auditoriums, garages, passenger terminals), highways and streets, conservation and development, electric and gas facilities, transit systems, and airfields.

percent in 1973, with the preponderance of benefits flowing to older people.[6]

Because the economy was growing so fast, it was not especially difficult for any level of government to pay for the added spending. Tax revenues grew even when tax rates were constant, because the sales, incomes, and property values on which the taxes were based were rising. At the federal level, growing incomes moved more people onto the income tax rolls and some

6. *Budget of the United States Government, Fiscal Year 1992*, table 15.5.

FIGURE 4-6. *Government Expenditures, by Level of Government, 1947–90*[a]

Percent of GNP

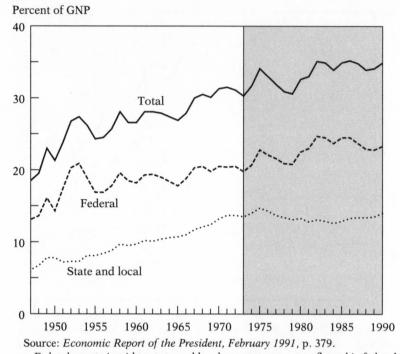

Source: *Economic Report of the President, February 1991*, p. 379.

a. Federal grants-in-aid to state and local governments are reflected in federal expenditures. Total government expenditures have been adjusted to eliminate this duplication.

into higher tax brackets, so income tax revenues tended to increase faster than GNP. Federal officials could win political plaudits for occasionally cutting tax rates and still have increasing resources to spend on federal services.

Most of the time government budgets were close to balance. The federal government actually ran modest surplus in its budget in a few years. Deficits were more frequent, but they were generally small, except during recessions. When economic activity slowed, tax revenues dropped and some antirecessionary spending increased. The excess of federal spending over revenue stimulated the economy and helped mitigate the effects of the recession. When growth resumed, tax revenues shot up again, recession-related spending declined, and the federal deficit dropped.

FIGURE 4-7. *Federal Debt Held by the Public, 1940–90*

Percent of GNP

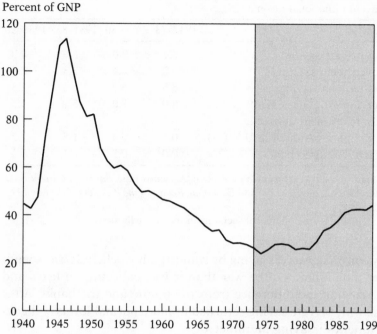

Source: *Budget of the United States Government, Fiscal Year 1992*, table 7.1.

Over the period from 1947 to 1973, federal deficits averaged less than 1 percent of GNP. Since the federal government was not borrowing very much, the debt rose fairly slowly, while GNP, pushed up by both inflation and real growth, increased more rapidly. Hence the ratio of the federal debt to GNP fell precipitously. As may be seen in figure 4-7, federal debt was larger than GNP in 1947, but had dropped to only 27 percent of GNP by 1973.

Saving, Investment, and Interest Rates

In the good news period, Americans were saving a significant portion of their income and investing it at home and overseas. During World War II, household saving was extremely high. Employment and wages went up, but there were not many big-ticket items to buy, so people put their money in the bank or lent it to the government by buying savings bonds. The government,

TABLE 4-1. *Net National Saving and Investment, Selected Periods,*
1947–90
Percent of national income

Item	1947–73	1974–80	1981–85	1986–90
Net private saving[a]	8.7	9.0	6.9	4.9
Government saving	−0.2	−2.1	−3.3	−2.6
Net national saving	8.5	6.9	3.6	2.3
Net domestic investment	8.0	7.0	5.1	4.7
U.S. investment abroad or				
foreign investment in U.S. (−)	0.5	0.4	−1.5	−2.7
Statistical discrepancy	0.0	−0.5	−0.1	−0.3

Source: National Income and Product Accounts tape, *Survey of Current Business* (1991), tables 5.1, 5.2; and *Economic Report of the President, February 1991*, table B-22.

a. Includes state and local social insurance contributions.

by contrast, was dissaving by running a big deficit. It was spending much more on the war than it was collecting in taxes and borrowing the difference from the public and the banks. After the war, private saving returned to more normal levels and government dissaving plummeted.

Over the whole period 1947–73, net private saving (saving by households and companies) amounted to about 8.7 percent of national income (table 4-1). Hence the nation as a whole was doing enough saving to finance net domestic investment of about 8 percent of national income and still add to American assets abroad.

In this period, the United States was a net exporter of capital; that is, American investments abroad grew more rapidly than foreign investments in the United States. Americans were drawing income from these foreign investments in the form of interest, dividends, and profits.

Anyone borrowing to make an investment should focus on the real interest rate, that is the nominal interest rate minus expected inflation.[7] Low real interest rates make investment,

7. For example, if prices were expected to be stable, hardly anyone would want to buy a house with a 15 percent fixed-rate mortgage. If prices, especially of housing, were expected to rise 10 percent a year, however, such a rate would look more attractive.

especially long-run investment, much more attractive, whether the investor is buying a house, building a factory, going to medical school, or financing a research and development project that is not expected to pay off for a long time.

In the good news period inflation was low, but so were nominal interest rates. After the price increases associated with World War II subsided, inflation settled down to rates that many other countries saw as enviable. Between 1948 and 1970, inflation averaged less than 3 percent a year. In 1971, when inflation exceeded 5 percent, President Richard M. Nixon, long an opponent of government price setting, ordered a freeze followed by price controls. Such a drastic response was evidence of how strongly Americans felt that low inflation was normal and desirable.

In the 1950s nominal short-term interest rates (such as the rate on three-month Treasury bills) were frequently even lower than the rate of inflation. In other words, real rates of interest were negative. In the 1960s and early 1970s, real short-term rates were only slightly higher, generally under 2 percent (figure 4-8). Long-term rates were also low by later standards. Moreover, government credit programs kept rates especially low for favored borrowers, such as homeowners and farmers.

When real rates are low, businesses and individuals can afford to be farsighted. They can borrow money to finance projects that have a moderate rate of return or that promise a high return at a distant date. When real rates are high, however, such projects are not attractive. It costs so much to borrow money that borrowers undertake only projects that promise a quick and high return. With hindsight, the investors of the good news period, both in the public and private sector, seem to have been more farsighted and less greedy for short-term returns than those of recent years. The explanation may not be in their moral character, but in the availability of funds at low interest rates.

Some Clouds on the Horizon

Not all the news was good. The growth of industry, population, and traffic brought serious environmental damage. Water quality deteriorated, and rivers and lakes in many parts of the country were disastrously polluted with sewage and industrial waste. Air quality worsened as a result of industrial emissions

FIGURE 4-8.   *Short-Term Real Interest Rates, 1948–90*[a]

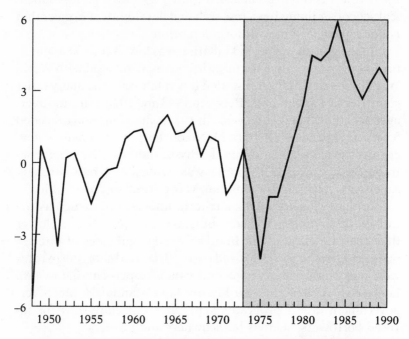

Source: *Economic Report of the President, February 1991*, tables B-2, B-71.
a. The rate on three-month Treasury bills minus the rate of inflation.

and the growing number of automobiles. Smog emerged as a serious problem, not only in the older cities of the Northeast, but also in the growing urban areas of the South and West—Atlanta, Denver, Phoenix, and, of course, Los Angeles.

Much of the growth in and around cities was helter-skelter urban sprawl. Moreover, the building boom was in the suburbs. Central cities, especially older ones, decayed as business and affluent population moved out, taking much of the tax base with them.

Worrisome social changes were also appearing. Divorce rates rose rapidly after World War II and continued to rise in the 1950s and 1960s. A rising proportion of children lived with only one parent. Concern about the stability and values of the American family was rising.

THE DISAPPOINTING YEARS

In October 1973, cuts in oil exports by Middle East oil producers pushed world oil prices up rapidly. Agricultural and other raw material prices were also rising around the world. Inflation surged in the United States and elsewhere. The Federal Reserve, in an effort to restrain inflation, tightened the money supply and sent interest rates up. The necessity of paying more for imported oil acted like a tax on consumers and businesses, leaving them less to spend on other purchases. The combination of shocks plunged the U.S. economy into its deepest recession since the 1930s. Unemployment reached 9 percent in May 1975.

Even when the economy began growing again, it did not replicate the surging success of the good news period. Unemployment came down slowly; inflation remained high. A second spurt of oil prices in 1979 precipitated another round of general price hikes.

Economists invented the word "stagflation" to describe simultaneous inflation and stagnant growth with high unemployment. Some of them talked about a "misery index" (the inflation rate plus the unemployment rate). The misery index was much higher from 1974 through 1980 than at any time during the good news period. (Nor has it been that high since 1980.)

The period 1974–80 was a tough time for economic policymakers because none of them knew how to deal with stagflation. Stimulative policies (cutting tax rates, increasing public spending, increasing the money supply, lowering interest rates) would reduce unemployment but were likely to aggravate inflation. Restrictive measures (higher tax and interest rates, lower public spending) would take the pressure off inflation but would probably raise unemployment. Even with hindsight, it is not clear what set of policies could have offset the inflationary impact of the oil shocks without creating substantial unemployment. Other industrial countries, battling the same forces with similar weapons, failed to find more satisfactory answers.

While economists and politicians argued about what to do, stagflation persisted. Public confidence in government, already reeling under the impact of the Vietnam War debacle and the Watergate scandals, eroded further.

The 1980s also started with a serious recession, precipitated by the Federal Reserve's determination (announced in late 1979) to squeeze the money supply and break the back of inflation. Interest rates jumped, spending and production faltered, and unemployment rose. The economy began to recover, then fell back into a "double dip" recession with unemployment rates reaching almost 11 percent at the end of 1982. All these negatives brought one big positive, however. Inflation returned to tolerable levels and stayed there, helped by declining oil and commodity prices and increasing international competition. Beginning in 1983, the economy experienced a long slow recovery that lasted until recession hit again in mid-1990.

In the period since 1973, the American economy has been struggling, its overall performance far less satisfactory than in the ebullient period from 1940 to 1973. It has been a period of slow average growth, weak productivity increases, widening disparities between rich and poor, low saving, rising debt, and accumulating problems that could make the future even more worrisome.

A Stagnating Standard of Living

After 1973, median family income stopped growing, declining in recession years and improving in recovery, but not resuming the upward march of the good news period (figure 4-1). Moreover, family income held up as well as it did partly because the average family had more earners. The wages of fully employed adult males actually declined when allowance is made for inflation. However, more women were working and their wages were rising. The number of young people at work also rose extremely fast, as the baby boom generation finished school and began to flood into the labor market. Between 1973 and 1990, increasing numbers of families had multiple earners, and the proportion of the total U.S. population that was employed rose from 41 to 48 percent (see figure 4-2).

Creating such a large number of jobs was a major success for the U.S. economy in the 1970s and 1980s. Less resilient European economies faced with similar increases in labor force participation were less successful in creating jobs. Their unemployment rates in the same period were considerably higher than those in the United States.

Although more people had jobs in the United States, the rapid productivity increase that had guaranteed rising incomes in the good news period petered out in the early 1970s. In the period from 1973 to 1979, productivity did not grow at all. When growth resumed, it was at a slow pace—only about 1 percent a year from 1979 to 1988, or about a third as fast as in 1960-69. The most worrisome problems were not in manufacturing, where productivity growth recovered significantly in the 1980s, but in the service industries that now included a large proportion of the labor force. Because output per worker was not rising at its previous clip, the average real earnings of workers were not rising appreciably either.

Shifting Income Distribution

Although the large income gains of the good news years were shared by all income groups, the smaller gains of the disappointing years were more concentrated at the high end of the income distribution (figure 4-3). From 1973 to 1979 income increases were modest at all levels, but the well-off did somewhat better than the poor. In the 1980s rising inequality was much more dramatic. The broad range of middle-income families were barely holding their own. Gains were greater for those at the top of the income distribution, while in the bottom fifth incomes actually declined.

An Increase in Poverty

The poverty rate reached its low point at 11 percent of the population in 1973 (figure 4-4). Poverty rates rose in the recession of 1974–75 and did not resume their downward path when the recession ended. The 1980s were even harder on the poor. Poverty rates rose in the 1980–82 recession and fell only slowly in the recovery of 1983–90. Then the recession that began in 1990 pushed poverty rates up again.

One bright spot was the continued improvement in the economic condition of the elderly. Much of the credit still went to social security: benefit levels were significantly increased in the early 1970s and then indexed to inflation. (Indeed, peculiarities of the indexing formula overcompensated the elderly for inflation in the early 1970s.) In addition, private pensions improved, the high interest rates of the 1980s benefited those living on prior savings, and the supplementary security income program (SSI) helped elderly persons whose other sources of income were inadequate. As a result, the poverty rate for people 65 years and over fell below the general poverty rate after 1982.

Poverty among children, however, surged in the late 1970s and has not fallen significantly since (figure 4-4). In 1990 more than one child in five lived in a poor family. Even more distressing was the apparent increase in extreme destitution. The number of children in families with incomes less than half the poverty level rose even faster in the 1980s than the total number of poor children.[8]

The increase in poverty among children in the 1980s was not confined to blacks or single mothers or the inner city. It was a general phenomenon cutting across race, geography, and type of family. The percentage increase in the number of children in poverty between 1979 and 1989 was higher for whites than blacks and much higher for Hispanics than for other groups in the population.[9]

Black-White Disparities

Progress in reducing economic disparities between blacks and whites stalled in the 1970s and has not resumed. The gap in earnings for black and white males has widened, not because wage rate disparities are growing, but because the proportion of black men who are employed has fallen relative to that for whites. Not only have black male unemployment rates been high, but an increasing proportion of black males are not even in the labor force.

This gloomy picture is not unrelieved. College-educated blacks have closed much of the gap between themselves and college-educated whites. The relative economic position of black women has improved more than the position of black men, although a substantially increased proportion of black women are supporting families by themselves. Indeed, a growing divergence has emerged in the black community between two-parent families, who are generally doing quite well, and single-parent families, who mostly are not.

8. Children's Defense Fund, *The State of America's Children, 1991* (Washington, 1991), pp. 23–24.
9. Children's Defense Fund, *State of America's Children*, p. 24.

Family structure and the position of women have changed dramatically in recent decades for blacks and whites alike. Women's contributions to family income have increased, and women are much more likely to head households and families than twenty or thirty years ago. The increase in female-headed households has been much greater for blacks than whites. (Forty-two percent of black families were headed by women in 1987, compared with 28 percent in 1970; 13 percent of white families were headed by women in 1987, 9 percent in 1970.) Roughly half of all children, and a much higher proportion of black children, now spend part of their growing-up years in a household without a resident father.[10]

Households headed by single mothers are much more likely to be poor or nearly poor than households with two parents, and they account for a substantial percentage of poor children, black and white. But households headed by black single mothers are nearly twice as likely to be poor as those headed by white single mothers. The differential growth of single families among blacks has contributed to lack of progress in narrowing income disparities.

The Collapse of Saving

A major piece of discouraging news did not begin until the 1980s: a worrisome plunge in American national saving. Government dissaving was slightly higher in the 1970s than in previous decades, largely because of the deep recession that followed the first oil shock, but private saving rates held at the levels of the good news period (table 4-1). Then, in the 1980s, the national saving rate dropped precipitously to less than half its previous level and stayed there.

The initial culprit was the rapid escalation of the federal deficit in the early 1980s. Part of this escalation was related to reduced federal revenues in the recession of 1980–82. The more worrisome part, however, was the structural, or underlying, deficit created by the tax cuts and spending increases of the early 1980s—a persistent gap between spending and revenues unrelated to the recession or recovery. Federal dissaving was

10. Bureau of the Census, *Statistical Abstract of the United States, 1989*, table 60; *Statistical Abstract, 1991*, tables 56, 58; and Children's Defense Fund, *State of America's Children*, p. 25.

partially offset by state and local surpluses in the mid-1980s, but these faded later in the decade. As a result of the federal deficit, debt held by the public began to rise faster than the economy was growing in the 1980s (figure 4-7).

The increase in public-sector dissaving would not have mattered so much if private saving had increased to compensate or at least held steady. However, especially in the second half of the 1980s, private saving declined as well (table 4-1). Both corporate and household saving fell off. In 1986–90, public-sector dissaving offset more than half of private saving, resulting in net national saving of only 2.3 percent of national income.

When American saving dropped in the 1980s, one might have expected two effects: a rise in interest rates and a drop in investment. Investors, bidding for a smaller pool of savings, would have to pay more to get funds, and interest rates would rise. At the higher rates, some investments would not be worth making and investment would fall.

Interest rates in the 1980s were in fact much higher than in previous decades, after allowance for inflation (figure 4-8). Many people are surprised to discover that interest rates rose so dramatically in the 1980s, because they forget to correct for inflation. They remember that nominal interest rates rose rapidly at the end of the 1970s and came down quickly in the early 1980s. However, inflation came down faster. Real rates of interest were far higher in the 1980s than in the 1970s.

Investment did not fall as much as one might have expected, however, because funds flowed into the United States from other countries, attracted by the high interest rates and attractive investment opportunities. Americans were able to use the savings of foreigners to offset the decline in their own. In the period 1986–90, foreign investment in the United States averaged 2.7 percent of GNP and financed over half of America's net domestic investment (table 4-1). Foreigners bought or built factories in Tennessee, hotels in Miami, and office buildings in Los Angeles, as well as investing in American stocks, bonds, and other securities. These investments created jobs and improved productivity, but they also required Americans to pay interest, dividends, and profits to people in other countries.

The result was a big switch for the United States. In the

good news period—indeed until the early 1980s—Americans had saved enough to finance their own investment and still invest somewhat more overseas than foreigners were investing here. In the 1980s, however, the United States imported foreign capital on a major scale. As a result, the United States, which had been one of the world's major creditors, instead became its largest debtor.

Deterioration of Infrastructure

Total government spending, which rose faster than GNP in the good news period, continued to do so in the 1970s and 1980s (figure 4-6). The increase, however, was for payments to individuals, especially older people, under social security and other entitlement programs—not for public investment. Beginning in the late 1960s, public construction declined as a percentage of GNP (figure 4-5). Moreover, evidence mounted that the nation's infrastructure was falling into disrepair.

The decline of new construction was not surprising. The move to the suburbs had slowed. The school population had stopped increasing and in many areas was actually declining. New approaches to medical treatment and efforts to contain hospital costs were reducing hospital stays and resulting in excess hospital capacity in many communities. The interstate highway system was substantially complete.

Lack of attention to repair and maintenance of public infrastructure was a more serious problem. Highways, bridges, and airports were aging and wearing out. Schools, hospitals, courts, jails, and public office buildings, especially in central cities and older communities, were becoming increasingly dreary, dilapidated, and in some cases unsafe. Water systems in older cities were expensively leaky and sometimes unhealthy.

Failure to maintain and replace deteriorating infrastructure can be costly. Old school buildings are expensive to heat, for example. Moreover, the costs are often borne by the private sector. Potholes and rough highways lead to expensive wear and tear on trucks and cars. Detours and delays on roads and airways are costly to travelers and shippers.

In the private sector, accounting practice requires that depreciation on long-lived assets be charged as a cost. This practice makes clear that there is a real cost to the use of structures and equipment and that even long-lived assets must eventually be replaced. In the public sector, depreciation is generally not charged and the costs are more likely to go unnoticed. However, maintenance and replacement cannot be delayed forever. The costs are simply put off and are likely to be higher if not addressed promptly.

Environmental Concerns

For much of the good news period, few people paid attention to the damage that unfettered growth and development were doing to the environment. As health hazards mounted, however, and dirty air and water became too unpleasant to ignore, the public began to demand political action to curb pollution and reduce dangers to health. An explosion of regulation followed, designed to improve air and water quality and control toxic wastes.

Some progress has been made. Some rivers and lakes are less polluted than they were. In some areas, air quality has improved; in others, deterioration has been halted. Yet the magnitude of the costs of long neglect of some serious hazards is just becoming apparent. Many problems are the legacy of earlier lax standards, and some are attributable to government itself. A monumental effort will be necessary to clean up the damage done by nuclear weapons production, find ways to deal safely with nuclear waste from power plants and other installations, restore areas contaminated by toxic wastes and prevent recurrence, reduce contamination of ground water, and improve air quality in cities. Public concern about the environment is high. The policy problems involve finding ways of sharing the cost equitably for past failures and designing prevention programs that minimize costs.

In short, the American economy in recent years has not been performing well. It has not been producing sustainable and widely shared growth in the standard of living. The next chapter turns to why the economic news has been so disappointing—and what might be done to bring back the good news.

FIVE   *What Went Wrong and*
What to Do About It

Since the good news period, in which almost everything went right in the American economy, ended in the early 1970s, much of the economic news has been disappointing. This chapter addresses two questions: Why did the good news peter out, and what can be done to brighten the economic future? Answering these questions involves delving into four economic mysteries: Why did productivity growth slow down, why did income inequality increase, why did national saving drop, and why did medical costs rise so rapidly? None of these questions has clear, unambiguous answers—they are genuine mysteries—but each yields clues to better performance in the future.

THE PRODUCTIVITY MYSTERY

It is hard to overestimate the importance of productivity growth to the economic future of Americans. Unless the population is spending more time working, the level of living can rise only if workers produce more goods and services per hour of work.

In the next couple of decades, a rising standard of living will depend on speeding up productivity growth. Unless immigration increases substantially, a relatively small number of people will enter the labor force because birthrates in recent years have been low. Moreover, beginning around 2010, the baby boom generation will begin to retire. To provide for all these older people, and to maintain a rising standard of living for themselves, the relatively small future work force will have to be much more productive than today's work force. Hence a crucial ingredient of a brighter economic future is making productivity grow faster.

Explaining the Drop

It was hardly surprising that the unusual postwar surge in U.S. productivity growth dampened somewhat by the 1960s. The dramatic reduction in productivity growth in the 1970s, however, took everyone by surprise. Something disturbing was happening, and not just in the United States. Europe, Japan, and the newly industrializing nations, whose productivity had been growing much faster than the United States in the postwar years, also experienced a sharp dip in productivity growth in the early 1970s. In general, however, their productivity growth recovered sooner and resumed a stronger upward trend than that of the United States.

Because the drop in productivity growth coincided with the substantial energy price increases that followed the 1973 oil embargo, energy costs were immediately blamed. Indeed, the rising energy prices in the 1970s probably contributed to the productivity slowdown, but energy is not a big enough part of the cost of production of most products to cause such a large and pervasive shift in productivity growth. Moreover, by the 1980s energy costs were falling relative to the cost of other goods and services, yet productivity growth did not resume its strong upward march.

Another suspect was the explosion of regulation that occurred, especially in the United States, in the 1960s and 1970s. Regulations reflected concern about health and safety hazards in the workplace, air and water pollution and toxic wastes, discrimination in hiring, pay, and promotion of women and minorities, and difficulties facing disabled workers. Compliance with the rules had substantial costs and undoubtedly exerted some drag on productivity as usually measured. The regulations contributed to higher quality of air or water, or more equal opportunities among workers, but those advantages do not show up in the gross national product, which is the basis of productivity measurement. Few analysts, however, see regulation as a major contributor to the productivity slowdown. In any case, the increases in regulation slowed in the 1980s.

The large number of inexperienced workers entering the labor force in the 1970s also probably slowed productivity growth. The young workers had more formal schooling than their elders, but they lacked on-the-job experience. Married women coming back into the labor force after raising children also had less work experience than men of the same age. By the 1980s, however, young workers were less numerous, women's career patterns looked more like men's, and the average experience level of the work force was rising.

Productivity often rises because new products or processes flow from research and development (R&D) undertaken by companies, universities, or governments. Growth in R&D outlays, which was vigorous in the good news period, slowed somewhat in the 1970s. Most of the R&D cutbacks, however, were defense related. Although military R&D has some spillover into civilian technology, it is not an effective way of increasing civilian productivity. Hence reductions in R&D growth probably made at most a minor contribution to the downturn in productivity growth, although the translation of research results into innovation in products and processes appears to have slowed in the 1970s in some important industries.

The productivity slowdown could not be attributed to less education, since the average years of schooling completed by workers was rising. Questions were raised, however, about the quality of education. Some declines in scores on standardized tests showed up in the late 1960s. Perhaps young people were watching too much television and not learning the skills they needed for success on the job. Perhaps the quality of instruction in schools or support from home had declined. Deteriorating quality of education, however, would probably have gradual effects. It could not explain the sharp drop in productivity increases that occurred in the 1970s, especially since most of the labor force had left school many years earlier.

Considerable effort has gone into parceling out the blame for the productivity crisis. Many factors appear to have played a role. However, neither separately nor together can they fully explain it. Some mystery remains.

How to Increase Productivity

The question that really matters for the economic future of America is not what happened in the 1970s, but what can be done now to increase productivity in the 1990s? A slew of study groups, task forces, committees, and commissions have addressed this question. Their prescriptions are beginning to have a familiar ring.

Most prescriptions call for drastic improvements in education and training, especially in basic literacy, mathematics and science, problem solving, and computer skills. There is overwhelming evidence that schools and vocational education programs in Europe and Japan prepare students much more effectively than American schools to work in a modern technological society. Many young Americans, especially in central cities, leave school without the reading and computation skills needed to hold any but dead-end jobs. Moreover, it is not just "bad" schools that are failing. Even students in "good" suburban schools do worse than their European and Japanese counterparts on tests of mathematical competence and scientific literacy.

Americans used to dismiss international comparisons on the grounds that American education was universal, while in many other countries educational opportunities were mostly for the elite. This rationalization, however, does not fit the current facts. Careful comparisons of students' scores on math tests at ages 9 and 13 in a substantial number of countries that have universal education show American youngsters falling behind early and staying behind.[1] Science test comparisons also show American

1. For example, American 9-year-olds averaged 58 percent correct answers to a set of math questions while 9-year-old Koreans averaged 75

13-year-olds with significantly less scientific knowledge than their counterparts in many other places, such as Korea, Taiwan, Switzerland, or Hungary.[2]

The economic case for upgrading skills and training does not rest on international comparisons alone. In the 1980s, the earnings of American workers with technical skills and higher education increased more rapidly than the earnings of workers without them, reversing the trend of the 1970s, when income disparities among education levels narrowed. There is considerable evidence that the demand for skills and education is outrunning the supply. Skill training and higher education appear to be investments with a high payoff, both for individuals and for society as a whole.

Another common theme of productivity prescriptions is the need to improve public infrastructure, especially roads, bridges, airports, and other modes of transportation. The deterioration and congestion of highways and airports is visible and annoying to many Americans and extremely costly in terms of lost time and repair bills. It is difficult to estimate how much improved transportation would contribute to productivity increases— some exaggerated claims have little foundation—but few doubt that improving infrastructure would boost productivity.

The improvement has to be done intelligently, however. Building more highways, especially in and around cities, is not likely to reduce congestion for long. Experience proves that highway capacity soon fills up and encourages urban sprawl, inefficient use of land, and increasing air pollution. Genuine improvements in transportation systems, especially in metropolitan areas, have to be financed in ways that discourage use of trucks that chew up the roads and deter both trucks and cars from using

---

percent. At age 13, the scores were 55 percent and 73 percent, respectively. Archie E. Lapointe, Nancy A. Mead, and Janice M. Askew, *Learning Mathematics*, report 22-CAEP-01, prepared for National Center of Education Statistics, U.S. Department of Education, and National Science Foundation (Princeton, N.J.: Educational Testing Service, February 1992), pp. 18, 83.

2. Archie E. Lapointe, Janice M. Askew, and Nancy A. Mead, *Learning Science*, report 22-CAEP-02, prepared for National Center of Education Statistics, U.S. Department of Education, and National Science Foundation (Princeton, N.J.: Educational Testing Service, February 1992), pp. 18, 84.

roads at peak hours (by charging them more). The proceeds should be used to modernize public transportation.[3]

Increasing R&D, especially the translation of scientific advances into new products and processes, also receives high priority in most reports on productivity. The United States has a strong record of achievement in basic science, but a far weaker one of moving from technological breakthrough to commercial success.

New management techniques are needed in a more competitive world. Big American companies pioneered mass production and assembly line methods in the 1920s. Now the emphasis has shifted to more decentralized management, greater emphasis on teamwork, worker creativity, and interaction with customers to ensure high quality and satisfaction. American companies, often overcentralized and top-heavy, have been struggling to adjust.

THE MYSTERY OF RISING INEQUALITY

The second mystery of recent economic history is: why did incomes become so much more unequal in the 1980s? As shown in chapter 4, the shift toward inequality was dramatic. The share of the least affluent dropped and that of the most affluent increased. Moreover, the very poor fared worst and the very rich fared best. Perhaps most worrisome, the long recovery from the recession of the early 1980s did not help low-income people nearly as much as previous recoveries had. Despite low unemployment rates and continuous, albeit slow, growth in total economic activity from 1982 to 1990, the proportion of children and working-age adults living in poverty remained surprisingly high. Thus the onset of the recession in mid-1990 made a bad situation even worse.

Why Inequality Increased

As with the productivity mystery, theories and culprits abound. Some blame President Reagan for cutting taxes of the rich and reducing benefits for the poor. Others blame foreign competition for eliminating middle-class jobs. Others point to

3. Kenneth A. Small, Clifford Winston, and Carol A. Evans, *Road Work: A New Highway Pricing and Investment Policy* (Brookings, 1989), chap. 7.

the breakdown of marriage, moral disintegration, or the rise of greed.

The decline in average welfare benefits did contribute somewhat to the worsening economic status of low-income families in recent years, although the decline began well before the Reagan era. In the 1960s, when concern for the poor was high, average welfare benefits increased faster than the cost of living. Since then, real benefit levels have eroded substantially. Between 1972 and 1990, real benefits for a welfare mother with three children and no earnings dropped about 23 percent.[4]

The only group whose average benefits did not decline were the elderly. Like social security, supplementary security income, the welfare program for the elderly and disabled poor, was indexed to the cost of living. Hence elderly and disabled beneficiaries fared better than younger welfare families.

Tax changes also played a limited role. Federal income tax rates were dramatically reduced in 1981, and the tax was restructured in 1986 to close loopholes and make tax rates on different kinds of income more equal. The net effect was to reduce the average tax burden on people with high incomes, but the effect at the bottom of the income scale was more complicated. The income tax changes of the 1980s removed most poor families from the income tax rolls altogether by raising the personal exemption and standard deduction and providing an earned income tax credit for low-wage earners with children. At the same time, however, payroll taxes for social security and medicare were rising, as were state sales taxes, so that the net tax burden on the working poor increased.

On balance, tax and income transfer changes in the 1970s and 1980s contributed to increasing inequality in the distribution of income—but not very much. The biggest increase in inequality occurred in incomes *before* taxes and transfers, espe-

---

4. Average monthly AFDC and food stamp benefits weighted by population of state. *Overview of Entitlement Programs, 1991 Green Book, Background Material and Data on Programs within the Jurisdiction of the Committee on Ways and Means: 1991 Edition*, Committee Print, House Committee on Ways and Means, 102 Cong. 1 sess. (Government Printing Office, 1991), pp. 1074–75.

cially in earnings of men. Hence the mystery of rising income inequality turns largely on the question of why men's earnings have become less equal.

The question is not a simple one. Inequality did not increase much in the 1970s, in part because some trends were offsetting each other. Younger workers—those baby boomers again— poured into the labor market, depressing the wages of their age group and putting a premium on experience. At the same time, the relative advantage of higher education declined, probably because the supply of educated workers had increased rapidly in earlier years.

In the 1980s, by contrast, the gap widened between the earn- ings of college graduates and of those who only finished high school. Men aged 25–34 with a high school education were earn- ing 11 percent less in 1987 than in 1979, after adjusting for infla- tion, while men with a college education were earning 8 percent more.[5] The greater monetary rewards for skill and education ex- plain at least part of the increasing disparity between rich and poor as well as the failure of blacks and other groups with low average skills and education to keep up. The explanation for this widening gap may relate to the rapidity of technological change or the deterioration of schools and skills—or both. In either case, an aggressive effort to improve the skills, education, and work incentives of less-skilled and less-educated young people and adults could be a policy "twofer." Such an effort could spur pro- ductivity growth and narrow income disparities at the same time.

Improving Skill and Training

The controversy over education reform is not over whether it is necessary, but over how to accomplish it and what it will cost. Educational reformers are divided into two camps. One group holds that a great deal of knowledge already exists about how to improve learning and teaching, but more resources will be needed to implement this knowledge in average schools.

5. Median earnings of year-round full-time workers. Frank Levy and Richard J. Murnane, "U.S. Earnings Levels and Earnings Inequality: A Review of Recent Trends and Proposed Explanations," *Journal of Economic Literature* (forthcoming, September 1992).

Higher pay will be necessary to attract more qualified people to careers in teaching, especially in science, mathematics, and computer technology. Funds are needed for retraining teachers and administrators, modernizing buildings and equipment, especially in the often dismal schools of older cities, and rewarding successful efforts of schools, teachers, and students.

The other group of reformers believes that significant improvements in education cannot occur within the current structure of public education and that additional spending would largely be a waste. They see public school bureaucracies as rigid, incompetent, and expensive. Overhead is so heavy that a relatively small amount of total funding is devoted to actual teaching at the classroom level. Teachers, principals, and administrators are not held accountable for educational results. Students and their parents are captive customers, unable to chose better education over worse except by moving to another community.

Many of those with negative views of the current American educational system believe that the solution lies in introducing market incentives into education. Some would do this within public school systems, for example, by allocating money to teachers to buy services (such as remedial reading specialists or psychological counselors) from central management only if they needed them. Students or parents would also be allowed to choose schools or programs within the public system that met their needs and produced results. Others take the more drastic view that education should be run by private enterprises. Parents would receive vouchers and shop for the best school for their child. Schools that failed to produce results would lose students and would either have to improve or go out of business. Proponents of choice and vouchers generally believe that more resources are unnecessary and might even retard reform.

Better measures of performance and more rewards for results must play a part in reform, but the claims made for the advantages of free enterprise in education have no firm basis in actual experience. The apparently superior performance of Japanese or European schools is not attributable to market incentives, except perhaps for higher teacher salaries. Drastic reform of the schools seems likely to require both new methods and additional money for salaries, training, and modernization.

Schools are only part of the story. Compared with Europe and Japan, the United States has paid little attention to the transition from school to work. Students not going on to college typically flounder around in the job market for several years without much idea of how to get a permanent job, what skills they need, or how to get them. Moreover, in a period of change, even those with skills may find themselves needing training for a new kind of career in midlife. A serious effort to increase productivity growth will require making retraining and additional education a normal part of working careers.

Reducing poverty and improving opportunities for those at the bottom of the income distribution is not just a matter of improving schools and training. It also requires offering better child care and health services and improving incentives to get off welfare. A major contribution could be made by reforming health financing to make health insurance available to low-income workers. The present system often penalizes welfare mothers who seek jobs by depriving them of medicaid coverage.

THE SAVING MYSTERY

The collapse of American saving in the 1980s raises serious concerns about the future health of the economy. If Americans are to make the investments necessary to raise productivity growth, they will have to either save more themselves or attract additional savings from foreigners.

Dependence on others for capital is precarious. Foreigners could lose confidence in the U.S. economy, stop investing here, and even sell some of the assets they now hold. American companies would find it harder and more expensive to raise funds. Interest rates could rise rapidly, perhaps throwing the country into recession. This disaster scenario is probably unlikely, but the continuation of high levels of foreign investment in the United States has costs and risks. Not only will foreigners end up owning big chunks of America, but Americans will pay increasing proportions of their output in interest, dividends, and profits to compensate foreign investors for the use of their countries' savings.

The Budget Deficit

The drop in American saving in the 1980s is actually only a partial mystery. Part of the fall was caused by a decline in private saving, which is quite mysterious, and part by an increase in public dissaving (mostly federal borrowing), which is not mysterious at all. The government was simply not taking in enough revenue to cover the cost of its services, so it had to borrow. Deterioration in state and local finances after 1984 also reduced national saving.

There has been a great deal of partisan wrangling about which political party bears responsibility for the federal budget deficit. Democrats generally blame the Reagan administration for cutting tax rates in 1981 and increasing defense spending rapidly in the early 1980s, although both policies were widely supported by Democrats as well as Republicans in Congress. Republicans like to point out that Reagan inherited a heavy tax burden and excessive domestic spending, and they blame Democrats for rejecting Reagan's efforts to cut domestic spending in the 1980s. There is obviously enough blame to go around.

As may be seen in figure 5-1, federal *domestic* spending did rise substantially between fiscal years 1960 and 1980—by almost 8 percent of GNP. Social security and medicare benefits accounted for a large share of the increase, but other domestic spending rose as well. The domestic spending increase was offset, however, by a decline of more than 4 percent in the proportion of GNP devoted to defense over the same period. Hence *total* spending increased less dramatically than domestic spending, by just under 4 percent of GNP between 1960 and 1980. Taxes went up even more modestly, and this increase was entirely because payroll taxes were increased to pay for rising social security and medicare benefits. Other taxes actually rose less rapidly than the economy was growing.

In the 1980s, income tax rate reductions and indexing of the tax system for inflation combined to cut the growth of federal revenues while defense spending growth accelerated. Domestic spending growth slowed, but not enough to offset the growth of outlays for defense and interest on the growing debt itself. High interest rates compounded the problem. Once the deficit was

FIGURE 5-1. *Federal Spending and Taxes, 1960–90*

Percent of GNP

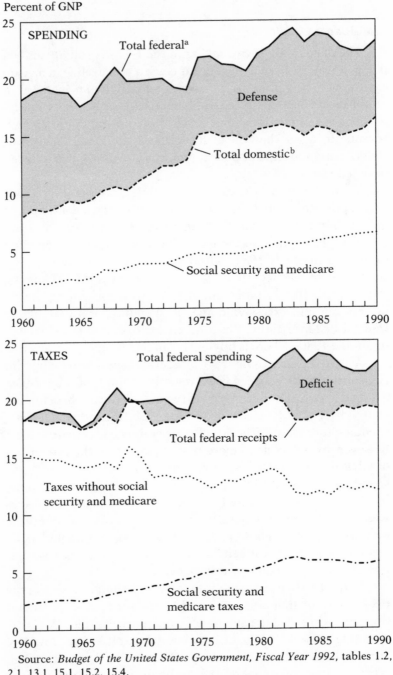

Source: *Budget of the United States Government, Fiscal Year 1992*, tables 1.2, 2.1, 13.1, 15.1, 15.2, 15.4.

a. Includes domestic, defense, and social security and medicare.

b. Includes social security and medicare, net interest, other federal payments to individuals, and other federal spending.

created, no one wanted to bear the pain of correcting it. The tax increases and spending cuts necessary to do so seemed more unpleasant than letting it continue.

Private Saving

The drop in private saving in the 1980s is much more of a mystery. Indeed, it contradicted what many people expected. Real interest rates were high in the 1980s, which many expected to encourage saving. Tax rates were cut on high incomes, which some thought might encourage saving. Tax benefits were offered to savers with individual retirement accounts (IRAs). Despite these incentives, private saving did not rise; it fell. Americans may have gotten used to the higher growth in their standard of living in the good news years. When the economy stalled, they tried to keep their consumption growing by saving less and borrowing more.

Increasing Saving

It is hard to know what public policies would increase private saving. Some favor increasing tax incentives for saving by giving more generous tax deductions for additions to IRAs or other types of accounts. Favorable tax treatment for private saving, however, reduces the government's revenue and adds to the federal budget deficit. Moreover, many of the people who take the deductions probably would save anyway. Hence the net addition to private saving attributable to the tax advantages may well be smaller than the increase in the federal deficit. If so, the result would be lower, not higher, national saving.

It is *not* hard to know what to do to raise public saving: reduce the federal deficit by raising taxes or cutting spending. It is just hard to muster the political support to do it.

The federal government has an unusual opportunity to increase the national saving rate in the 1990s and well beyond, because the social security system will be running substantial annual surpluses. Running surpluses to build up the reserves in the system is appropriate because benefit payments will escalate in the next century when the baby boom generation retires. The trouble is that the government is currently borrowing these reserves to cover expenses that have nothing to do with social security, such as paying soldiers and maintaining national parks. The rest of the government is running such a big deficit that the Treasury has to borrow all of the increase in the social security reserves—and a lot more besides—just to pay the bills.

It is not illegal for the Treasury to borrow from social security. On the contrary, the law actually requires the social security system to invest in government securities.[6] If the government's deficit were eliminated, the social security system would have to go into the bond market to buy existing government bonds now held by the public (including banks, companies, and foreigners). These purchases would reduce the federal debt held by the public. The system's reserves would add to the pool of funds available for private business and state and local governments to use for investment. Interest rates would fall, and additional productive projects, both private and public, would be undertaken. The new investment would raise future national income.

Why not let social security finance productive investment directly by buying stocks and bonds in the market? Because that would concentrate too much power in the hands of the government. No good would come of making the government a big shareholder in private companies or the principal owner of state and local bonds. It makes much more sense to use social security reserves to reduce the national debt and thus indirectly to release funds for new investment. The only way to accomplish this, however, is to reduce the government deficit.

THE MEDICAL COST MYSTERY

In the last three decades, the cost of medical care in the United States has skyrocketed (figure 5-2). Health care's share of the total economy more than doubled between 1965 and 1990. The United States spends substantially more per capita on health care than other industrial countries. Moreover, the higher spending does not seem to buy better health. Neither average life expectancy nor infant mortality compares favorably with these measures in other industrial countries.

---

6. Private pension funds also invest part of their reserves in Treasury securities because they are regarded as virtually risk free.

FIGURE 5-2. *Health Expenditures, 1950–90*

Percent of GNP

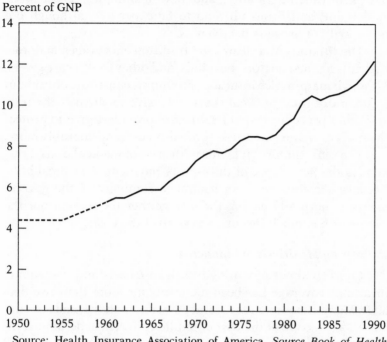

Source: Health Insurance Association of America, *Source Book of Health Insurance Data* (Washington, 1990), table 4-3; and *Economic Report of the President, February 1991*, table B-1.

The continuous rise in American health care spending is straining many parts of the economy. Business is finding employee and retiree benefits increasingly costly and is cutting back on employer-provided coverage. Over 33 million Americans, many of them children, are now without adequate health insurance. Meanwhile, public costs are escalating rapidly. Medicaid costs are putting heavy pressure on state and local budgets. Both medicare and medicaid are increasing federal spending and making it more difficult to reduce the federal deficit. (See chapter 9 for further discussion.)

Why Medical Costs Are Rising

The growth of medical costs reflects multiple forces all pushing in the same direction at the same time. The population is aging, and older people are heavy users of medical care. Technology is advancing rapidly, and new techniques, procedures, equipment, and drugs all tend to be expensive, although not necessarily of proven effectiveness.

The litigious American legal tradition encourages malpractice suits against doctors, hospitals, and other health care givers. Although malpractice insurance premiums constitute only about 1 percent of total medical costs, defensive medicine—the tests and other procedures that health care providers give to protect themselves against lawsuits—probably costs considerably more.

The most important factor in the rise of medical costs, however, is the prevalence of third-party payment of medical bills. Because someone else—an insurance company or the government—is normally paying the bill, neither the patient nor the caregiver has much incentive to control the cost.

Reforming Health Care Financing

Concern about mounting health care costs and inadequate insurance coverage has been mounting for more than two decades. Many states and the federal government have made strenuous effort to control the cost of public care. The federal government, for example, developed elaborate and quite effective controls on hospital reimbursement rates under medicare. These controls have reduced the rate of increase of hospital spending under the federal medicare program, but hospitals have tended to transfer the costs to private payers. The private sector, in turn, has tried to hold down escalating costs by turning to managed care and various kinds of health maintenance organizations. Efforts have been made to hold down the proliferation of high-tech equipment through regional planning. None of these fragmented approaches, however, has done the trick. The cost of insurance continues to escalate, and more people are being forced off the insurance rolls.

The result is a growing consensus that a national solution is necessary. Even business groups that used to fear public solutions are now calling for some sort of overarching national health plan that would control costs by setting fees and reimbursement rates for health providers and extend coverage to those who are not now covered by private plans. (Options are discussed further in chapter 9.)

THE NATIONAL DILEMMA

There is no reason to think that the United States cannot achieve sustainable and widely shared growth in its standard of living. However, it will take a will to change course and strong commitment to a new set of policies. The most important are:

—Drastic reform of education and training to increase the productivity of the labor force and improve opportunities for those with low skills;

—Investment in comprehensive modernization of infrastructure, especially transportation;

—Increased investment in research and development and new technological applications;

—Reforming the health system to control costs and extend coverage to the uninsured;

—Moving the federal deficit into surplus to add to national saving and channel more resources into private investment.

In fact, a large consensus supports these reforms—in principle. The problem is not what to do, but how to do it and who should take the lead. The federal government cannot take on all these activities without an enormous increase in federal taxes, which the public is unlikely to support. Nor does the federal government have the managerial and administrative capacity to execute this whole agenda effectively. Parts of it require experimentation and adaptability to particular local and regional situations. State and local governments are much better suited than the federal government to undertake major parts of it. It is time to take a new look at American federalism and how responsibilities are divided between the states and the federal government.

SIX *The Evolution of American Federalism*

A theme of this book is that the federal government has taken on too much responsibility and should return some of its functions to the states. A clearer division of responsibilities between the states and the federal government could make both levels operate more effectively.

This position, however, appears to fly in the face of history. For much of the twentieth century, power has flowed toward Washington and the functions of federal and state government have become increasingly intertwined. Why did this happen? Are the reasons for the blurring of distinctions between federal and state government still valid today?

CHANGING VIEWS OF FEDERALISM

To the Founding Fathers, the division of responsibility between the states and the federal government was a crucial issue with high emotional and intellectual content. Most of them believed that the states should retain a large measure of autonomy. Their experience with the English crown made them nervous about lodging too much power in any central government. Life under the Articles of Confederation, however, demonstrated that the national government could not function effectively if its powers were too narrow or if it depended on state contributions for revenue. Hence the drafters of the Constitution gave the federal government limited but quite specific powers, including the power to levy and collect taxes. To reduce misunderstanding, they later added a Tenth Amendment stating explicitly that "the powers not delegated to the United States by the Constitution, nor prohibited by it to the States, are reserved to the States respectively, or to the people."

The Tenth Amendment seems clear enough, but the Constitution itself was a document drafted by a committee. It contained some language suggesting more comprehensive powers for the national government, such as the statement that Congress should provide for "the general welfare." Hence the Constitution did not permanently settle the controversies about which level of government should have which functions. It did, however, create a framework for debating and resolving conflicts between the federal government and the states that has stood the test of more than two centuries.

From 1789 to about 1933, all levels of government were small by modern standards, but the states were clearly more important than the federal government, except possibly in time of war. Moreover, the two levels of government usually ran on separate tracks, each in control of its own set of activities. Scholars called the arrangement "dual federalism."

From the Great Depression through the 1970s, all levels of government expanded their activities, but power shifted to Washington. The federal government took on new responsibilities, and the distinction between federal and state roles faded. Scholars talked about "cooperative federalism."

By the beginning of the 1980s, the drive for centralization had peaked, and power began shifting back to state capitals. No new concept emerged, however, of how responsibilities should be divided. The current era has been called a period of "competitive federalism," meaning the federal government and the states are competing with each other for leadership in domestic policy.[1]

SMALL GOVERNMENT AND DUAL FEDERALISM

The national government created by the Constitution was charged with defending the new country and dealing with the rest of the world. It sent diplomats to foreign capitals, dealt with the Tripoli pirates, fought the invading British, invaded Mexico, and warred with Spain. Above all, it kept the nation together despite the disaster of the Civil War and the tensions of reuniting North and South.

In the nineteenth century, much of the national government's attention was devoted to acquiring territory and encouraging its settlement and development. Washington granted land to settlers and developers and encouraged the entry of new states. It fostered trade and interstate commerce and subsidized canals and railroads. It arranged the delivery of mail, managed the national currency—often with conspicuous lack of success— and encouraged the growth of banks.

Sometimes economic development shaded into what is now called "social policy." For example, new states were given land grants for public schools. In 1862 the national government endowed land grant colleges to teach agriculture and the "mechanical arts" and later (in 1890) granted these institutions a modest annual subsidy. The federal government also engaged in a few public health activities early in its history, such as maintaining hospitals for merchant seamen. In general, however, social policy matters such as education, health, and aid to the poor were the concern of state and local governments or private charity.

By the end of the nineteenth century, the excesses of big business and the human cost of unfettered profit seeking were arousing public anger and creating pressure for federal intervention. Antitrust laws reined in monopolies. In the early years of the twentieth century, the "muckrakers" pointed to scandalous health, safety, and labor practices, and the Progressive movement fought for corrective action. The federal government

1. John Shannon and James Edwin Kee, "The Rise of Competitive Federalism," *Public Budgeting and Finance*, vol. 9 (Winter 1989), pp. 5–20.

moved to regulate food adulteration, child labor, and other abuses. Progressives had more success in some states, however, than they did in Washington, in part because the courts took a narrow view of the role of the federal government.

Dual federalism was never absolute. Even in the nineteenth century, there were instances of federal-state cooperation on law enforcement or public works and modest overlaps of functions.[2] Scope for intertwining of functions was minimal, however. The national government was remote from most citizens and its activities were few.

Until the early years of the twentieth century, the modest scope of the federal government did not require a broad-based tax system. Revenues from customs duties and the sale of public lands amply covered peacetime spending. Indeed, there was often a surplus of funds. A federal income tax, although used briefly to help finance the Civil War, was thought to be unconstitutional.

In 1913 the Constitution was amended to permit the federal government to levy an income tax, and the Federal Reserve System was created to put banking and credit on a more solid basis. The Federal Reserve was eventually to give Washington a powerful set of tools for influencing the economy by controlling money, credit, and interest rates. The federal income tax was ultimately to finance a huge expansion in federal activities. Both developments, however, lay in the future. In the 1920s, conservatives dominated Washington and the federal role remained limited. In 1929 total federal spending was under 3 percent of GNP. States and localities spent almost three times as much as the federal government.[3]

TWO REASONS FOR FEDERAL GROWTH

In the Great Depression of the 1930s, the federal government took on new responsibilities, and its budget grew rapidly. Federal domestic functions continued to expand after World War II, even as America's worldwide responsibilities were growing

2. Daniel J. Elazar, *The American Partnership: Intergovernmental Cooperation in the Nineteenth-Century United States* (University of Chicago Press, 1962).

3. *Economic Report of the President, February 1991*, pp. 310, 379.

FIGURE 6-1.   *Domestic Government Expenditures, Selected Periods, 1947–90*

Percent of GNP

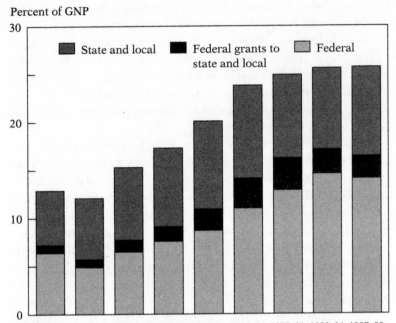

Source: *Budget of the United States Government, Fiscal Year 1992*, tables 1.2, 3.1, 15.2.

(figure 6-1). By the late 1950s federal domestic outlays exceeded amounts spent by state and local governments from their own sources.

This escalation of Washington's role is often seen as a single juggernaut of centralization, sweeping power toward Washington. Two sources of growth, however, should be distinguished. One was the evolving conviction, dramatically reinforced by the Great Depression, that new national institutions were needed to strengthen the economy and perform functions that states could not be expected to perform on their own. This conviction prompted a wave of institution building that included both purely federal activities and joint federal-state efforts.

A second source was the escalating perception, reinforced by the civil rights movement, that states were performing badly even in areas that almost everyone regarded as properly assigned to them. Frustrated with the states, reformers urged the federal government to augment state spending and redirect state and local priorities. The result was a rapid proliferation of grants to states—and directly to their localities—designed to strengthen their capacities and influence their decisions.

BUILDING NATIONAL INSTITUTIONS

The Great Depression brought the economy close to collapse and radically altered the role of the federal government. The stock market crash of October 1929 presaged an economic free-fall. Factories and businesses closed, millions of workers lost their jobs, the banking system tottered, and citizens were frightened and insecure. President Herbert Hoover, unable to stem the tide of economic disintegration, lost the 1932 election in a landslide to Franklin D. Roosevelt, who proclaimed a "New Deal."

The Roosevelt government took over in mid-crisis. Its first task was to get the economy functioning again. To stop a disastrous run on the banks, the new administration briefly closed all banks and then reopened them under new rules. Over a quarter of the labor force was unemployed. The federal government handed out emergency relief. It put people to work on a vast array of projects from building dams and schools to painting murals and recording folk music. The federal government created institutions to buy home and farm mortgages from hard-pressed banks and reschedule them so families could retain their homes and farms. It lent money to businesses on favorable terms and prodded industry to produce and hire. These efforts helped to revive the economy, but unemployment was still high at the end of the 1930s. Only World War II got the economy booming again.

The Great Depression revealed weaknesses of a highly unregulated and decentralized economic system. It changed the public's view of the desirable role of the federal government and impelled the president and the Congress, despite initial resistance from the Supreme Court, to create federal institutions and programs to reduce the chances of economic disaster striking again.

Since the weakness of the banks had nearly brought the economy to a halt, the architects of reform were eager to strengthen banking, credit, and financial systems. Deposit insurance, bank and thrift regulation, and housing and farm credit institutions greatly increased the stability of the banking system and made it easier for business, homeowners, and farmers to obtain credit.

Agricultural distress and rural poverty, aggravated by the worldwide collapse of commodity prices, bad weather, and poor farming practices, dramatized the need for regional development and agricultural assistance. The federal government brought electricity to rural areas, built dams to supply power and control floods, supported agricultural prices, and aided large and small farmers.

A strong national commitment to a freer world trading system also began in the Depression. The U.S. Smoot-Hawley Tariff Act of 1930 had set off a tariff war that was widely blamed for precipitating the worldwide depression. The United States took the lead in reversing course and working with other nations for reciprocal lowering of trade barriers.

The human suffering of the Great Depression, brought on by massive unemployment and falling wages, created public pressure for permanent institutions to protect individuals from the impact of economic catastrophes beyond their control. The institution builders responded with two different approaches: social insurance and welfare programs.

Social Insurance

Social insurance enables the population to pool certain risks, such as losing income because of unemployment, disability, retirement, or death of the family breadwinner. Workers pay a portion of their wages (usually matched by their employer) into a government fund while they are working and are entitled to benefits when they retire or when specified disasters strike. Social insurance taxes are analogous to insurance premiums or private pension contributions. Those who have contributed long enough do not have to prove that they are destitute to get benefits—just that they are disabled or unemployed or retired. Unlike welfare, there is no means test and no shame in accepting benefit checks.

The social security system. The biggest social insurance program, social security, evolved from small beginnings in

1935 into a strong and extremely popular national institution. Workers covered by social security pay a tax on their earnings, matched by their employer. In return, when they retire they receive a pension whose level is related to their past earnings. Benefits are paid to disabled workers and to survivors if the worker dies. The social security system gradually expanded to include virtually all workers; benefits increased over several decades. In 1965 medical benefits for the elderly (the medicare program) were added to the social security system.

Unemployment insurance. Unlike social security, the unemployment insurance system, set up in response to the massive unemployment of the Great Depression, was a joint state and federal effort. The federal government assisted the states in setting up unemployment insurance funds and established many of the rules, but left the level of contributions and benefits up to the states themselves.

Social insurance proved a popular, successful, and enduring concept. Part of its popularity relates to the contributory feature and the specificity of the benefits. People feel they are paying for identifiable benefits that will be there if they need them. They object less to social insurance taxes than to the general taxes that support government services whose benefits are widely dispersed and hard to identify.

Welfare Programs

Social insurance was a response to the economic hardships of the 1930s, but could not be an immediate solution. Workers had to build up eligibility for future benefits. Meanwhile, people were destitute. State welfare programs were totally swamped. To meet part of the need, the federal government put in place a set of means-tested welfare programs to provide income to some poor families and individuals. The elderly, blind, and disabled and women supporting children were entitled to payments if they could prove that they had inadequate means. Like the social insurance programs, these welfare programs were "entitlements": people who met the requirements specified in the law were entitled to benefits. However, the benefits were paid out of general government revenues, not out of a fund to which beneficiaries contributed.

The welfare programs were expected to become less necessary as social insurance coverage widened and gave people who were unemployed, retired, or disabled a means of support. The hope was that widows with children would increasingly be covered by survivors' benefits under social security; the subsequent growth of the number of divorced and single women with children was not anticipated.

Social insurance did reduce poverty, but the means-tested programs did not disappear. Indeed, rising concern about low-income families (especially women with children) prompted not only the expansion of aid to families with dependent children (AFDC), but the addition of other federal means-tested programs in the 1960s and 1970s, including food stamps, expanded housing assistance, and medicaid (the joint federal-state program that finances medical care for low-income people).

Funding and responsibility for welfare programs were shared by federal and state governments (and in some states, by local governments as well) in complex and interlocking ways. In general, the federal government made the rules about who would be eligible for benefits on what conditions, but states set the actual benefit levels and administered the funds. The federal government matched the money paid out by the state according to a formula that gave more federal money (per dollar of state money) to poorer states. Benefit levels varied substantially, with poor states generally providing low benefits despite proportionately higher assistance from the federal government.[4]

Stabilizers for the Economy

Social insurance and welfare programs not only provided income to individuals and families facing economic disaster, they also made economic disaster less likely. If economic activity dropped off sharply, the downward spiral would be cushioned, since individuals drawing social insurance benefits and welfare would be able to buy necessities and pay their rent or mortgages. This increased purchasing power would bolster the income of producers and prevent layoffs of workers and forced sales of

---

4. The food stamp program is an exception. The funds are federal and the benefit formula is the same in all states.

homes. Thus both welfare programs and social insurance would act as automatic stabilizers for the economy.

Other National Initiatives

Growing federal activities cost money, but Washington was not short of funds. Federal income tax rates were raised to high levels to finance World War II, and withholding was introduced in 1943. Both personal and corporate taxpayers got used to paying a significant portion of their income to the federal government. Moreover, in the good news period (see chapter 4), personal incomes and business profits rose rapidly. Even after taxes, almost everyone was doing well. The federal tax system was generating so much revenue that new programs could be funded while tax rates were reduced. Moreover, the share of GNP devoted to defense declined gradually after the Korean War buildup in the early 1950s. Domestic spending growth could be accomplished without commensurate increases in the overall federal share of GNP.

By 1960 the federal government's budget for domestic programs alone had grown to 8.1 percent of GNP.[5] Between 1933 and 1960, the role of the federal government had changed from that of a minor player on the domestic government scene to a major one.

INFLUENCING AND REFORMING THE STATES

Despite the growth in some types of federal programs, many types of public services were still considered very much the business of the states until the early 1960s. Elementary and secondary education, health services, police and fire protection, sanitation, social services, and most other direct services to citizens were still viewed as overwhelmingly state and local matters.

Only occasionally did Washington intervene in these areas to further an objective deemed worthy of national attention. For example, the federal government began giving the states grants for vocational education programs in high schools as early as 1917. In the late 1950s, when the Soviet Union's Sputnik launch

5. *Budget of the United States Government, Fiscal Year 1992*, p. 182.

focused attention on technical education, Washington set up grant programs designed to improve science, mathematics, and language teaching in the schools (the National Defense Education Act). These "categorical" grant programs accumulated slowly over the years and then exploded in the 1960s and 1970s.

In the 1960s, President Lyndon B. Johnson's Great Society programs reflected mounting dismay that the states were not performing effectively and were shortchanging the poor, urban dwellers, and minorities. States and their local governments were seen as lacking the means and the capability to provide services in a modern society. Federal programs were designed explicitly to change the way states performed their own functions.

The Sad State of the States

Dissatisfaction with the states had been building for several decades, starting with the Great Depression. State governments were unable to cope with the nation's economic crisis. Reformers turned to the federal government, which responded with a blizzard of new activity. Some began to regard the states as anachronisms that might eventually fade from the American governmental scene. Political scientist Luther Gulick declared in the depths of the Great Depression, "It is a matter of brutal record. The American State is finished. I do not predict that the states will go, but affirm that they have gone."[6]

The challenges of World War II further augmented the powers of the federal government, and activists continued to turn to Washington to deal with perceived needs of the postwar economy for housing, hospitals, and an interstate highway system. Bashing the states was a popular sport. Writing in 1949, Robert S. Allen characterized state government as "the tawdriest, most incompetent and most stultifying unit of the nation's political structure."[7]

6. Quoted in Ann O'M. Bowman and Richard C. Kearney, *The Resurgence of the States* (Prentice Hall, 1986), p. 4.

7. Quoted in Morton Keller, "State Government Needn't Be Resurrected Because It Never Died," in Thad L. Beyle, ed., *State Government: CQ's Guide to Current Issues and Activities, 1989–90* (Washington: Congressional Quarterly, 1989), p. 174.

By the early 1960s, when national concern about minorities and the poor was rising, states were seen as perpetrators of discrimination. The southern states were overtly racist, defiant of federal efforts to desegregate schools and other public facilities and to ensure the participation of all races in the political process. Moreover, the indictment of states went far beyond the South and beyond issues of race and poverty. As Frank Trippett put it: "One glaring truth of the times is that most of the perplexing domestic problems confronting the country today would not exist if the states had acted."[8] Terry Sanford, a former governor of North Carolina, concurred: "Because many groups and people have encountered evasion of duty by the state, they have felt that they had no choice but to try the road to Washington. The trek to Washington could have been expected, for government is not static." Sanford, a strong believer in the necessity and feasibility of state reform, conceded, "If nothing much can be done, then indeed the states will soon be finished."[9]

The weakness of state government involved both the executive and legislative branches. In many states, governors had relatively few powers and short terms of office. They had small staffs composed of political appointees with limited professional qualifications. They presided over executive branch departments that were often fragmented, poorly organized, and staffed with bureaucrats who had limited training and education and few of the tools and skills of modern government. The office of governor itself often attracted "good-time Charlies" at the end of careers in the private sector. Abler politicians gravitated toward the federal government, where there was more scope for their talents.

State legislatures, before the reforms that began in the 1960s, were far from models of strong democratic institutions. Legislatures often met for only a few weeks every other year. Members served part time, were paid little, and were dependent on their primary jobs. They had hardly any staff, usually not even clerical support.

8. Frank Trippett, *The States: United They Fell* (New York: World Publishing, 1967), p. 2.
9. Terry Sanford, *Storm Over the States* (McGraw-Hill, 1967), pp. 36, 1.

Rural areas typically dominated the legislature. Cities and their growing suburbs were underrepresented, as were minorities and lower-income people. Rural overrepresentation was often built into state constitutions that required equal representation of sparsely populated rural counties and densely populated urban ones. In many states, entrenched rural interests had simply prevented reapportionment of the legislature for years or even decades. In 1962 Tennessee had not reapportioned its legislature since 1901. Eight states had not redistricted in more than fifty years, and twenty-seven states had not redistricted in more than twenty-five years.[10] "Some of the resulting inequalities were spectacular. In 1960 the five largest counties in Florida had half the population and 5 of 38 Senate seats; the Senate districts ranged in population from 10,000 to 935,000. Los Angeles County had 40 percent of California's population and only 1 of 40 seats."[11]

Although larger, richer states, such as New York and California, tended to have more capable governments, states in general did not inspire confidence. They were seen as "errand boys" of the federal government, helping to carry out policy formulated at the national level. Even this role diminished as the federal government increasingly bypassed states and dealt directly with local governments.

The Civil Rights Revolution

The civil rights movement, which gathered steam in the 1950s and reached a climax in the 1960s, profoundly altered the relationship of the federal government to states and localities. The Civil War, nearly a century earlier, had freed the slaves and amended the Constitution in an attempt to guarantee equal rights for all races. In fact, however, blacks, especially but not exclusively in the South, were denied basic political rights (including the right to vote), excluded from public facilities and services, discriminated against in employment, educated in separate and inferior schools, denied access to higher education, and otherwise relegated to second-class citizenship and economic deprivation.

10. Sanford, *Storm over the States*, p. 35.
11. Malcolm E. Jewell, "What Hath *Baker v. Carr* Wrought?" in Beyle, ed., *State Government*, pp. 85–95, quotation on p. 86.

After World War II, growing outrage on the part of blacks and a rising proportion of the whole population swelled into a national movement. State segregation laws were challenged in the federal courts under the U.S. Constitution, and the federal government passed legislation spelling out equal rights in greater detail. In 1954, in *Brown* v. *Board of Education*, the Supreme Court rejected the idea that separate schools could be regarded as equal. Gradually, schools, universities, and other public facilities were desegregated, but not without dramatic confrontations between state and federal officials.

Enforcing civil rights laws involved the assertion of federal authority in schools, parks, hospitals, restaurants, hotels, and other facilities that had not heretofore been seen as areas of federal concern. Efforts to right past wrongs involved increasingly complex intrusion on state and local autonomy. Even after legal segregation of school systems was abrogated, for example, de facto racial segregation remained because blacks and whites lived in different neighborhoods. As a result, the courts searched for ways of achieving racial desegregation of the schools by redrawing school boundaries and busing children out of their neighborhoods.

The War on Poverty

The civil rights movement, by focusing attention on economic as well as political deprivation of minorities, aroused concern about the general prevalence of poverty. Americans rediscovered that even in their prosperous country a large population, in both rural and urban areas, lived at the margin of subsistence. The poor included low-wage workers in agriculture, manufacturing, and service industries, dwellers in depressed areas such as Appalachia and the Mississippi Delta, native Americans, and Hispanics. Blacks were only about a quarter of the poor.

In 1964 President Johnson called for a war on poverty. He sent an avalanche of proposals to Congress designed to change the lives of the poor in a variety of ways. Most were enacted in a frenzy of legislative activity that rivaled the early days of the New Deal.

The investment strategy. The strategists in the war on poverty saw the poor as mired in a cycle of poverty from which they were ill equipped to escape because of bad health, lack of skills, and lack of experience, both in the workplace and in the political process. They emphasized an investment strategy of providing the poor not with money, but with services that would help adults and children break out of the poverty cycle. Providing these services to the poor involved federal intervention in a whole range of government functions previously regarded as state and local prerogatives.

A prime example of the investment strategy was the Head Start program, whose premise was that because poor children came to school less ready to learn than middle-class children, they fell behind and were never able to catch up. Head Start provided intensive preschool education to improve the skills, health, and nutrition of low-income children and enhance their chances of succeeding in school. Other federal programs provided special services for low-income youngsters to help them progress through school, get jobs, or go to college. (Principal programs included follow through, teachers corps, title I of the Elementary and Secondary Education Act, job corps, neighborhood youth corps, and upward bound.) In addition, neighborhood health centers offered health resources in areas with few doctors and medical facilities. Legal services helped poor people obtain redress of grievances and claim benefits to which they were entitled under the law. Community action programs, perhaps the most controversial of all, tried to mobilize the poor to be more effective politically in their own behalf.

Some programs were intended to demonstrate that a broad range of coordinated services could turn a deteriorating area into an improving one. Riots in Los Angeles, Detroit, Washington, and other big cities in the late 1960s directed attention to blighted urban areas. Urban renewal, model cities, and other programs channeled federal funds directly to city governments.

The investment strategy of the war on poverty involved a great many programs and projects. Most were relatively small, however. They reached only a minority of the population in poverty and did so in ways that were usually too fleeting to make a life-changing difference.

Income strategy proposals. Many people concerned about the poor thought the investment strategy was too slow and indirect. Better education, beginning in preschool, might eventually enable poor children to earn more, but four-year-olds would not be in the labor force for about fourteen years. Meanwhile, they were growing up amid deprivation and blight. What the poor needed most urgently was money—a means of paying for necessities such as food, housing, and medical care.

Some scholars and politicians were attracted to the idea of a guaranteed income, sometimes known as a negative income tax (NIT). They believed that existing welfare programs were demeaning and undermined incentives to work because family earnings were deducted from the welfare grant. A poor family was effectively subject to a 100 percent tax on earnings. Under an NIT, a family with no income would be guaranteed a minimum income and would be encouraged to work because the grant would be reduced (or "taxed") by less than their earnings.[12] Thus an NIT would both provide income for families who could not work and encourage those who could work to do so. Some thought that such a system could be administered by the Internal Revenue Service (IRS). Families with adequate incomes would pay positive taxes, those with low incomes would get checks (or negative taxes), and only the IRS would know the difference.

The NIT was an intriguing idea, although it would have been more expensive and difficult to administer than its initial proponents imagined. Efforts to convert President Johnson to the idea failed. He was committed to the investment strategy, especially to opening educational opportunities for poor children, and had little interest in reforming welfare. In any case, by the end of Johnson's presidency in 1968, escalating defense spending was squeezing domestic programs. The NIT was ruled out by cost as well as philosophy.

To the surprise of most liberals, President Richard M. Nixon endorsed a welfare reform proposal in 1969 that bore striking

12. Suppose the guarantee were $8,000 a year for a family of four. If the tax rate were 50 percent and the family earned $4,000, the grant would be reduced by $2,000 and the family would end up with a total income of $10,000.

resemblance to an NIT. Nixon proposed guaranteeing a minimum income to all families and encouraging work by reducing the guarantee less than the amount of earnings. The proposed guarantee level was below the welfare benefits paid to AFDC families in urban states, but above the benefits in the South. The proposal would have put a national floor under income for the first time and substantially benefited low-wage workers.

President Nixon's family assistance plan, as it was called, passed the House of Representatives twice, but was defeated in the Senate by a coalition of conservatives, who thought it too generous to the poor, and liberals, who thought it not generous enough. The idea survived in the supplementary security income program, which was essentially an NIT for people who were elderly, blind, or disabled.

Despite the absence of an income strategy in the war on poverty and the failure of Nixon's reform, welfare programs grew rapidly in the 1960s and even faster in the 1970s. Collectively, these programs had a much bigger impact on federal budgets than the investment strategy programs. AFDC increased as larger proportions of the poor applied for aid and benefit levels rose. Medicaid, passed at the same time as medicare, provided health benefits for many low-income families, especially those eligible for AFDC. The food stamp program, which went to a broader group of low-income people than AFDC, grew rapidly. Public housing and other housing subsidies for low-income families increased.

The Proliferation of Grants

Federal activism in the 1960s and 1970s spread from poverty and civil rights into many other areas. Turning to Washington for help became routine. Pollution, transportation, recreation, economic development, law enforcement, even rat control, evoked the same response from politicians: create a federal grant. National concern shifted from one problem to another, but existing grants were never terminated. The result was an accumulation of more than 500 categorical programs, each with detailed rules, formulas for matching and distributing the money, bureaucracies charged with carrying out and overseeing the program, and beneficiaries and professional groups with an interest in perpetuating and enlarging the grant.

Some critics worried that the pervasiveness of federal grants reduced state and local autonomy. Others were more concerned that the proliferation of grants allowed state and local authorities to do whatever they wanted and send the bill to the federal government.

States and cities learned to tailor their budgets to maximize federal funding. Unfortunately, they sometimes neglected more routine activities. According to New York City Mayor Edward I. Koch:

Left unnoticed in the cities' rush to reallocate their budgets so as to draw down maximum categorical aid were the basic service-delivery programs. . . . New roads, bridges, and subway routes were an exciting commitment to the future, but they were launched at the expense of routine maintenance to the unglamorous, but essential, infrastructure of the existing systems.[13]

Another problem was that less affluent jurisdictions often lacked the savvy or the staff to take full advantage of the federal largesse, especially when it took the form of project grants for which they had to compete. Wealthier states and cities were able to put together more sophisticated or better-documented project proposals.

Revenue Sharing

In 1964, Walter Heller, chairman of the Council of Economic Advisers in the Johnson administration, proposed "revenue sharing" to channel federal money to the states without the detailed specifications of categorical grants. Revenue sharing responded to several problems besides the growing concern about categorical grants. Needs for public services at the state and local level were rising more rapidly than revenues; state and local revenues grew more slowly and fell more heavily on low-income people than the federal income tax; federal income tax revenues tended to rise faster than the need for federal spending; and poor states could not be expected to bring services up to acceptable national levels without help. Revenue sharing would address all these concerns by channeling a portion of federal income tax receipts

13. Edward I. Koch, "The Mandate Millstone," *The Public Interest*, no. 61 (Fall 1980), p. 43.

to the states—no strings attached—with low-income states receiving disproportionate shares.[14]

President Johnson rejected the revenue sharing proposal. He favored social programs managed directly by Washington or categorical grants with tight federal controls. During his administration, the number of categorical grants exploded, and the revenue sharing idea remained buried deep in the White House files.

President Nixon, however, was attracted to revenue sharing, which fit well with his "New Federalism" philosophy of increasing state autonomy (see chapter 7). His proposal, known as general revenue sharing, was enacted in 1972 with the enthusiastic support of state and local politicians.

General revenue sharing funds were specified in the law, not tied to the federal income tax. The money was disbursed under a formula that benefited poor states disproportionately. The money was divided into two parts, one to be spent at the state level and one to be "passed through" to local governments. The earmarking of a local share reflected the fears of mayors that they would not get enough money if they had to lobby for it in their state capitals. Rules were also introduced to try to prevent the recipients from substituting federal money for existing funding.

That revenue sharing was popular with state and local officials is hardly surprising. It provided financial support and made no onerous demands. It was not, however, equally popular with members of Congress, who preferred more control over how federal funds were used. Hence categorical grant programs continued to grow in the 1970s, while revenue sharing did not.

14. Specifically, the federal government would annually deposit funds equal to 2 percent of the federal income tax base in a trust fund for the states. The money would be divided among the states on the basis of population and could be used for any purpose except highways (a trust fund for highways already existed). Each state would work out its own way of sharing the money with its local governments. Task Force on Intergovernmental Fiscal Cooperation, "Strengthening State and Local Government: A Report to the President of the United States," November 11, 1964 (unpublished). The task force was chaired by Joseph A. Pechman. President Johnson, allegedly angry because Heller had leaked the proposal to the *New York Times*, refused to release the report.

The Reagan Revolution

President Ronald Reagan was a conservative former governor of California with strong views about the role of government, at both the federal and state levels. He won a landslide victory over President Jimmy Carter in 1980 after vociferously attacking federal domestic spending in his campaign and advocating deep cuts in federal income taxes, more defense spending, and a balanced budget. Within weeks of taking office, Reagan confronted Congress with a drastic budget proposal involving major increases in defense spending, deep cuts in domestic programs, and reductions in federal income taxes over a three-year period. Congress, awed by the electorate's evident desire for change and skillfully manipulated by Reagan's energetic director of the Office of Management and Budget, David Stockman, passed both the tax and budget proposals with astonishing rapidity.

Reagan administration budget policy profoundly influenced the future of relations among federal, state, and local governments. As Richard Nathan and Fred Doolittle put it:

The cuts made in grants-in-aid in Reagan's first year in office were historic. This was the first time in over thirty years that there had been an actual-dollar decline in federal aid to state and local governments. The cuts produced a 7 percent reduction for fiscal year 1982 in overall federal grants-in-aid to state and local governments . . . . This amounted to a 12 percent decline in real terms.[15]

Federal grants were both reduced and restructured. Categorical programs were grouped into block grants that gave state and local governments more latitude in spending the funds. The Reagan cuts fell heavily on the poor, especially the working poor, and hit cities more dramatically than states.

Most of the reductions in domestic spending came during Reagan's first year in office. Subsequent requests for additional cutbacks met increasing opposition from Congress and the public. Some of the funds cut in the initial reductions were later restored, and modest increases in grants occurred late in the 1980s. Huge federal deficits, however, kept downward pressure

15. Richard P. Nathan, Fred C. Doolittle, and Associates, *Reagan and the States* (Princeton University Press, 1987), p. 4.

on federal spending, especially discretionary spending, which is easier to control than entitlements. Very few new federal grant programs were created in the 1980s. Federal aid to state and local governments (as a percentage of GNP, the federal budget, or state and local spending) stayed well below the level of the late 1970s. The pattern of increasing state and local dependence on federal grants had been broken.

One of the casualties of the Reagan revolution was general revenue sharing. Opponents pointed out that huge deficits left no federal revenue to share. Congressional support for revenue sharing was weaker than support for the categorical programs that affected identifiable clients and professional groups. First the state and then the local components of revenue sharing were eliminated.

Unexpectedly, the Reagan cuts energized state and local governments. The cuts created what Richard Nathan has called "the paradox of devolution." With less federal help, states, and to some extent localities, were forced to strengthen their own capacities and resources to meet the rising social problems of the 1980s. The federal pullback came at a fortunate moment— after two decades that had greatly enhanced states' ability to move into the breach.

THE STATES RISE TO THE CHALLENGE

The dissatisfaction with state government that reached a crescendo in the 1960s not only prompted an explosion of federal activity, it also brought a wave of reform in the states themselves. Goaded partly by the federal government and partly by pressure from their own citizens, states took steps to turn themselves into more modern, responsive, competent governments. By the time the Reagan revolution of the 1980s thrust new responsibilities on them, state governments were far more ready to rise to the challenge than they would have been two decades earlier.

Executive Branch Reforms

One theme of the state reform movement was strengthening the capacity of governors to provide state leadership. Colonial antagonism toward a strong executive had left a legacy of state constitutions with strict separation of powers between the executive and legislative branches and carefully circumscribed gubernatorial powers. As a result, governors frequently lacked the tools and resources needed to lead a modern state.

Presidents, of course, faced the same problem for the same reason, but in the first half of the twentieth century there were major improvements in the organization and staffing of the White House. For example, the Bureau of the Budget (later called the Office of Management and Budget) was created in 1921 and the Council of Economic Advisers was established in 1946.

Efforts to improve the capacity of governors came later. In the early 1960s, many governors served only two years, not long enough to articulate and carry out a strategy for state action. Many were lame ducks, prohibited from succeeding themselves. Many governors had limited powers of appointment; other state officials were directly elected and had their own power bases. Many appointments were made by boards or commissions whose members were elected, controlled by the legislature, or served fixed terms from which they could not be removed. Governors often had neither the authority nor the staff to prepare an executive budget for the legislature. Indeed, states' chief executive officers frequently lacked powers that CEOs of corporations would regard as absolutely essential to leadership and effectiveness.

A common reform was shifting to longer terms, as well as lifting restrictions on succession. In 1955 governors had four-year terms in only twenty-nine states. By 1988 the number had risen to forty-seven. In the same period, the number of states in which governors were barred from a second successive term dropped from seventeen to three.[16]

Other reforms shortened the ballot and reduced the number of independently elected state officials. A widely quoted report by the Committee for Economic Development in 1967 urged that only two state executives, the governor and the lieutenant governor, be elected and that they run as a team from the same

16. Thad L. Beyle, "From Governor to Governors," in Carl E. Van Horn, ed., *The State of the States* (Washington: Congressional Quarterly, 1989), pp. 35–36. The holdouts for two-year terms are all small New England states: Rhode Island, New Hampshire, and Vermont. Kentucky, Virginia, and New Mexico still bar succession.

party, like the president and vice president. More states now elect the governor and lieutenant governor as a team, but the effort to reduce the number of elected officials has met with only modest success. Over the period 1960–80, the number of states electing four or fewer executives rose only from three to nine.[17] Between 1956 and 1988, the number of separately elected officials besides the governor dropped from 709 to 514, still an astonishingly high average of more than 10 per state.[18] Some governors obtained more formal powers of appointment and removal. Longer terms also tended to increase the governors' control of boards and commissions whose members are appointed for fixed terms.

During this era there were also substantial increases in the size and professional qualification of staffs, with the average size of the staff rising from eleven in 1956 to forty-eight in 1988.[19] Governors also created budget and planning offices charged with developing an executive budget reflecting the governor's priorities, formulating longer-term plans for the state and its government, and monitoring the effectiveness of state programs. Almost all governors now prepare an executive budget and submit it to the legislature with extensive backup analysis.[20]

In this period, state agency officials, like the staffs they supervised, became visibly more professional. They had more degrees and were more likely to be career civil servants. State officials became more diverse, although women and minorities are still underrepresented at the top of state governments.

Governors themselves have been described as a "new breed"—younger, better educated, less likely to be lawyers, more likely to seek careers in public service. Many of them have been state legislators or agency executives. Many go on to the U.S. Senate or to other federal positions.[21]

17. Bowman and Kearney, *Resurgence of the States*, chap. 2.
18. Beyle, "From Governor to Governors," p. 36.
19. Beyle, "From Governor to Governors," p. 36.
20. By 1983, the governor shared the power to put together an initial budget with the legislature in only three states (South Carolina, Texas, and Mississippi). Bowman and Kearney, *Resurgence of the States*, p. 61.
21. Larry Sabato, *Goodbye to Good-Time Charlie: The American Governorship Transformed*, 2d ed. (Washington: Congressional Quarterly Press, 1983).

None of these changes, of course, guarantees that governors will be successful or effective. Leadership qualities are in short supply at the state, as at the federal, level. Judgment and luck, as well as formal qualification and power of office, play an enormous role in determining a governor's effectiveness. Nevertheless, an able governor now has far more opportunity in most states to formulate and carry out policy than he (and now occasionally, she) would have had in the early 1960s.

Reforming the Legislative Branch

Reform of state legislatures in the 1960s came partly in reaction to stronger governorships. The American system of separation of powers invites such swings of reformist zeal from one branch to the other. The creation of the Congressional Budget Office in 1974 was in part the result of the strengthening of the presidential budgetmaking capacity in the 1960s and creation of policy analysis staffs in cabinet agencies. Congress needed professional help in responding to the increasingly sophisticated budget presentations of the president's staff. State legislatures, after the strengthening of governors' offices, found themselves in a similar position.

A more urgent impetus, however, came from the Supreme Court. In *Baker* v. *Carr* (1962), the Court indicated its willingness to hear cases in which voters in a state claimed that malapportionment of their legislature denied them equal protection of the laws under the Fourteenth Amendment to the U.S. Constitution. Then in *Reynolds* v. *Sims* (1964) the Court took the startling position that equal protection required *both* houses of the state legislature to be apportioned on a population basis, despite the fact that the U.S. Constitution specifies equal representation for all states in the U.S. Senate regardless of population. States rapidly reapportioned their legislatures to conform to the court's principle of "one person, one vote." This redrawing of the lines, now repeated after every census, brought a new and far more diverse group of legislators to state capitols and added pressure for other kinds of reform.[22]

---

22. Alan Rosenthal, "The Legislative Institution: Transformed and at Risk," in Van Horn, ed., *State of the States*, pp. 69–102.

In general, reapportionment favored metropolitan areas, especially growing suburban communities. It put urban problems on state agendas and eventually led to increased state aid to cities. Political fallout varied. Democrats gained more seats in the Northeast and Midwest, but Republicans benefited in the South.[23]

At the same time, the work load of legislatures was increasing. Short sessions every other year were no longer adequate. More and more states found that part-time citizen-legislators were unable to cope with the demands of modern state activity. Legislative sessions were lengthening, and pay had to be raised to compensate legislators who were now spending a substantial part of their working hours on state business. Legislatures also began to demand better working conditions and more professional and clerical assistance. Members needed staff both to service constituent requests and to work on increasingly technical legislative matters. Committees became more active and utilized more professional staff.

Strengthening State Revenue Systems

In recent years, states have strengthened and diversified their revenue systems. States and localities generally have become much less dependent on property taxes, which used to be almost the sole source of local revenue and an important one for states as well. Sales taxes, whose bases have been significantly broadened, now bring in more total revenue than property taxes. More important, many states and some cities have begun to rely more heavily on income taxes. States and localities have also turned for revenue to a broad range of fees and charges designed to make the actual users of state and local services pay a larger share of the costs. Between 1960 and 1990, property taxes dropped from 37.7 percent to 21.8 percent of the revenue state and local governments raised from their own sources, while individual income taxes grew from 5.7 to 14.8 percent and fees and charges grew from 16.8 to 28.9 percent.[24]

23. Jewell, "What Hath *Baker v. Carr* Wrought?"
24. Advisory Commission on Intergovernmental Relations, *Significant Features of Fiscal Federalism*, vol. 2: *Revenues and Expenditures* (Washington, 1991), p. 132.

The trend to broader-based state and local revenue systems in this period has been called "one of the most dramatic turn-arounds in the annals of American public finance."[25] Although states and localities are still hard-pressed to raise enough revenue to pay for the services demanded by their citizens, their revenue systems are stronger, more responsive to economic growth, and less regressive than they were a few decades ago.

Moreover, states and localities have raised more revenue, despite frequent protests from taxpayers. State and local revenue, exclusive of federal grants, has gone up from 7.6 percent of GNP in 1960 to 10.3 percent in 1990.[26]

Meanwhile, the federal government's fiscal strength has declined. There was a time when revenues from the highly progressive federal income tax tended to grow faster than the economy as a whole. Rising incomes moved taxpayers into higher brackets, where they paid a higher proportion of their income in tax. Even if people's real income had not increased, inflation tended to increase the government's revenue by pushing taxpayers into higher brackets. This phenomenon was known as "bracket creep."

In 1981, however, the federal income tax was made less progressive by reducing rates on high incomes. Moreover, beginning in 1985 the tax brackets were adjusted for inflation to remove bracket creep. Hence federal revenues no longer grow faster than the economy. Moreover, except for social security payroll taxes, federal revenues as a share of GNP have been declining. Federal revenues (excluding social security taxes) fell from 15.4 percent of GNP in 1960 to 12.0 percent in 1990 (see figure 5-1).

MANDATES

The federal government's own fiscal weakness has not made it any less eager to tell states and localities what to do. Indeed, when its ability to make grants declined, the federal government turned increasingly to mandates as a means of controlling state and local activity without having to pay the bill.

Mandates take several forms. Some are direct orders to

25. Shannon and Kee, "Rise of Competitive Federalism," p. 14.
26. *Budget of the United States Government, Fiscal Year 1992*, table 15.1.

states and localities to comply with certain rules (such as waste-water treatment standards) or face civil or criminal penalties. Some of them are cross-cutting requirements routinely attached to federal programs (compliance with antidiscrimination rules or minimum wages). Others impose conditions on a whole system (access for disabled people to mass transit or schools) as a condition of receipt of federal grants for any part of the system.

In the 1960s and early 1970s, when federal money was flowing to states and localities in increasing amounts, the recipients expressed little concern about the conditions attached to grants. As money tightened, however, and mandates became more pervasive and expensive, state and local officials became increasingly strident in criticizing federal mandates. David R. Beam noted that the character of the dialogue went from "cooperative" to "other 'c' words—like compulsory, coercive, and conflictual."[27] Complaints from the state and local level were hardly ever about the purposes of federal mandates, which were acknowledged to be laudable. Rather, they were about the federal government's asserting the authority to write complex and costly regulations that then had to be implemented by states and localities. "Cities and states feared that they were becoming the 'field hands of federalism'—simply, tools for implementing national policy directives in environmental protection, race, sex and age nondiscrimination, handicapped access and education, bilingual education, health planning, and other areas."[28]

Mayor Koch expressed the views of many state and local officials on the receiving end of multiple federal mandates in a satirical list of rules that appeared to be followed by the "mandate mandarins" in Washington: (1) "Mandates solve problems, particularly those in which you are not involved"; (2) "Mandates need not be tempered by the lessons of local experience"; (3) "Mandates will spontaneously generate the technology required to achieve them"; (4) "The price tag of the lofty aspiration to be served by a mandate should never deter its imposition on others."[29]

27. David R. Beam, "On the Origins of the Mandate Issue," in Michael Fix and Daphne A. Kenyon, eds., *Coping with Mandates: What Are the Alternatives?* (Washington: Urban Institute Press, 1990), p. 23.
28. Beam, "Origins of the Mandate Issue," p. 23.
29. Koch, "The Mandate Millstone," pp. 43–44.

Although state and local governments have challenged federal mandates in the courts in recent years, they have generally lost. New mandates continue to be added. Among the most costly, although the cost has been shared by the federal government, are mandates for additional services to low-income families under medicaid.

Mandates add to citizen confusion about who is in charge. When the federal government makes rules for state and local officials to carry out, it is not clear to voters who should be blamed, either when the regulations are laxly enforced or when the cost of compliance is high.

WHITHER FEDERALISM?

In the last decade, the tide of centralization has turned and the balance of power has generally shifted from the federal government toward the states. The states have strengthened their capacity for governance and their revenue systems, while the federal government has found itself overstretched and short of funds. The intertwining of roles, however, has not diminished. Federal grant programs have received less funding, but their number remains huge—a recent publication lists more than 600 federal grant programs for state and local government.[30] Mandates have been used to enforce federal policy when funds were limited. No new concept of federal and state roles has yet emerged. The next chapter explores alternatives for the future relationship between levels of government.

30. U.S. General Accounting Office, *Federal Aid: Programs Available to State and Local Governments*, HRD-91-93FS (May 1991).

SEVEN   *Rethinking Federalism*

Thus far I have argued that, for a variety of reasons, the division of tasks between federal and state government urgently needs to be reexamined.

—Global interdependence requires the federal government to pay more attention to international affairs, so states must play a stronger role in domestic policy.

—The policies needed to revitalize the economy, which include eliminating the federal deficit and increasing public investment in skills and infrastructure, cannot all be undertaken by Washington without a federal tax increase too big to be either likely or desirable.

—Top-down management by the federal government is unlikely to bring about needed change in education, skill training, and other areas where reform is essential.

—Some objectives, though, such as reform of health financing and control of medical costs, cannot be attained by states on their own.

110

—Increased competence and responsiveness of state government have weakened the rationale for many federal programs.

    —Citizens' lack of trust in government, especially at the
federal level, is exacerbated by confusion over which level of
government is in charge of what and how tax money is being
spent.

THREE SCENARIOS

What might happen to the division of responsibilities between states and the federal government in the 1990s? Three
scenarios illustrate the possibilities.

The Eighties Continued

In the early 1990s, federal policy continued to be dominated
by a distressing legacy of the 1980s: the huge structural deficit
in the federal budget. The deficit, combined with politicians'
perceptions that the public would not tolerate increased federal
taxes, required restraining discretionary spending and avoiding
new federal initiatives. Rising social security reserves and declining defense spending provided some offsets, but escalating
costs of medical care and bigger outlays for interest on the growing debt kept pushing spending up.

The first scenario assumes that federal tax and spending
policies continue on the basic tracks established in the 1980s
without important changes. Using similar assumptions, the Congressional Budget Office projects the federal deficit continuing
at high levels into the next century (table 7-1). To be sure, the
deficit is projected to decline as the economy recovers from the
recession of the early 1990s and the deposit insurance crisis is
resolved, but beginning in 1997, the deficit again begins to rise
faster than total output.

The surprising resurgence of the federal deficit expected at
the end of the decade is not caused by declining revenues, which
remain close to 19 percent of gross domestic product (GDP). Nor
is it caused by future Congresses voting new spending programs
or adding to old ones: the projections assume continuation of the
stringent caps on discretionary spending imposed by the budget
agreement of 1990. Nor is social security to blame. Social security outlays remain about constant at 4.8 percent of GDP—the

TABLE 7-1. *Federal Budget Projections, Fiscal Years 1992–2000*[a]
Percent of GDP

Item	1992	1993	1994	1995	1996	1997	1998	1999	2000
Revenues	18.6	18.8	19.1	19.1	19.1	19.0	19.0	19.1	19.1
Outlays									
Defense and domestic discretionary	9.4	8.7	8.1	7.7	7.5	7.3	7.2	7.1	7.0
Entitlements and mandatory spending									
Social security	4.9	4.8	4.8	4.8	4.8	4.8	4.8	4.8	4.8
Medicare and medicaid	3.4	3.6	3.7	4.0	4.2	4.4	4.7	4.9	5.2
Other	3.9	3.7	3.5	3.4	3.2	3.3	3.2	3.2	3.1
Deposit insurance	1.1	1.1	0.5	-0.2	-0.6	-0.4	-0.2	-0.2	-0.1
Net interest	3.4	3.4	3.5	3.5	3.5	3.6	3.6	3.6	3.7
Offsetting receipts[b]	-1.2	-1.1	-1.0	-1.0	-1.0	-1.0	-1.0	-1.0	-1.0
Total	24.9	24.2	23.1	22.0	21.6	22.0	22.2	22.5	22.7
Deficit	6.3	5.4	4.0	2.9	2.5	3.0	3.2	3.4	3.6

Source: Congressional Budget Office Testimony, Statement of Robert D. Reischauer, Hearings before Subcommittee on Economic Stabilization, House Committee on Banking, Finance, and Urban Affairs, April 7, 1992.
a. Assumes no changes in tax or spending policies and enforcement of caps on discretionary spending in the Budget Enforcement Act of 1990.
b. Includes contributions from allied nations for Operation Desert Storm.

influx of retiring baby boomers starts about a decade later—and growing social security surpluses continue to offset part of the general fund deficit.

The sole reason that federal spending is projected to rise faster than GDP (without any economic or policy changes) is that rapidly increasing medical care prices will continue to push up spending for medicare and the federal share of medicaid. The cost of these two programs is projected to rise from 3.4 percent of GDP in 1992 to 5.2 percent in 2000.

This scenario assumes that politicians continue to view federal tax increases as politically risky. Congress and the president tinker with the tax system, but do not enact major revenue increases. They enact a few revenue-losing changes in the name of incentives for saving or investing (for example, a cut in income tax rates for long-term capital gains or more generous individual retirement accounts). These are offset by some revenue gainers in the name of fairness or financing infrastructure (a surcharge on millionaires or another nickel or dime of gasoline tax). Without a significant redefinition of the federal role, however, it is hard to imagine either a president or Congress mustering the political courage to increase revenue much above 19 percent of GNP.

Similarly, Congress and the president go on tinkering with federal spending. They continue to reduce defense spending while adding modest new domestic initiatives (some education, some child care, some low-income housing) but no major commitments. Continued concern about the deficit and fear of major tax increases also precludes significant new spending for health finance reform. Without the ability to fund new programs, the federal government goes on using mandates to affect state and local policy. Without effective medical cost control, both federal and state health programs steadily grow more expensive. The cost of private health insurance rises and more people are uninsured.

Meanwhile, under this scenario, the states keep struggling with rising demands for services, the escalating cost of medicaid, and additional federal mandates. They raise taxes and fees as much as necessary to stay afloat but are not able to finance major new initiatives. The division of tasks between states and the federal government remains muddy. Citizens continue to be confused about whom to blame for unsolved problems. Activist groups and state and local officials go on lobbying Washington for additional spending on everything from preschools to mass transit but have only limited success. The economy, still suffering from insufficient saving and high real interest rates, continues to limp along.

"The eighties continued" is definitely not a scenario for healthy and widely shared growth in the standard of living. With private investment levels no higher than those in the 1980s and no serious effort to improve schools, job training, or public infrastructure, productivity growth does not accelerate. Family incomes grow slowly, if at all. Moreover, escalating medical costs lower the amount of income working people can spend for other purposes—either because employers pay lower wages in the face of the rising cost of medical benefits or because workers have to pay the bills themselves.

If no aggressive measures are taken to improve the education, skills, or health of low-skilled workers, their situation will probably continue to deteriorate relative to that of the highly skilled and educated. The federal debt will continue to increase, requiring high annual interest payments that reduce funds available for federal programs. Moreover, with the federal government borrowing a substantial fraction of the nation's saving, the United States will remain dependent on foreigners for capital and will have to pay them substantial sums (in interest, dividends, and profits) for the use of that capital.

Paul Krugman has sketched out some of the implications of a similar scenario, which he calls "drift":

If the domestic U.S. economy in the year 2000 may look fairly similar to its current state, the international economy—and the role of the United States in that international economy—will almost surely look quite different.

In the first place, foreigners will own quite a lot of America. Net foreign claims on the United States will be something like 20 percent of GNP, with interest and dividends on these claims nearly 2 percent of national income. . . . It would not be surprising if, by the year 2000, foreign firms account for 25 percent of U.S. manufacturing production and own 45 percent of our banking sector.

The widespread foreign ownership will be a blow to traditional views of America's place in the world. . . . By the year 2000, an increasingly unified Europe will have a larger GNP than America's and Japan will have a GNP that in dollar terms is 80 percent or more of the U.S. level. . . . So by many measures the United States will have sunk to the number three economic power in the world.[1]

Krugman expects that Americans will simply allow this deterioration to occur and will not muster the political energy needed to get the country on a more positive track.

Back to the Sixties

The second scenario assumes that the electorate, refusing to accept "diminished expectations," demands federal action, or that some calamity, economic or political, propels an activist president into the White House with a supportive majority in Congress. With the energy of a Franklin D. Roosevelt or a Lyndon B. Johnson, the new president puts together an aggressive program of federal spending and tax increases and steers it through Congress. The federal government launches major new grants to both state and local governments—to improve skills, subsidize low- and middle-income housing, modernize infrastructure, and reform the schools. Washington churns out checks for programs and projects all over the country, along with guidelines, rules, and reporting requirements. The federal government also enacts either national health insurance or some less expensive health financing plan that subsumes medicaid.

All this federal activity raises the share of federal spending to perhaps 26 percent by the end of the decade (more if full national health insurance is enacted). Federal domestic spending rises by more than total spending because defense spending continues to decline. Taxes are raised, not only to pay for the increased federal activity, but to narrow the deficit. A combination of increases in taxes on payroll, sales or value added, energy, and income raises federal revenue from 19 to 25 percent of GDP and cuts the deficit to 1 percent of GDP. Even this huge assumed rise in the federal tax burden does not move the federal budget to surplus. Some economists argue, however, that major increases in public investment make borrowing more defensible under this scenario than in the 1980s, when public investment was low.

The combination of federal grants and relief from rising

---

1. Paul Krugman, *The Age of Diminished Expectations: U.S. Economic Policy in the 1990s* (MIT Press, 1990), p. 193.

medicaid costs enables states and localities to reduce taxes. While federal revenue rises faster than GDP, state and local revenue rises more slowly. Policy action shifts back to Washington, along with intense lobbying by myriad interest groups, including state and local governments, for a piece of the additional federal funding. Able people seeking careers in public service, whether as civil servants, political appointees or elected officials, gravitate to Washington, because that is "where the action is."

If the "back to the sixties" federal programs were well designed and executed, they might energize the economy, accelerate productivity growth, and put the United States back on the track of higher expectations and leadership in the world community. The risks, however, are large. It is not clear that the federal government has the capacity to manage new programs that intervene in so many aspects of community life. Can Congress and the president exercise leadership in initiating so many domestic reforms and oversee their execution at the same time they are dealing with all the problems of leadership in an increasingly complex and interdependent world? Can they find a way between the twin dangers of loose federal controls that invite misallocation of funds and rigid controls that are often inappropriate in local situations? Past experience suggests strong doubts.

The most serious impact of pervasive federal activism might be on the quality of state and local government and on citizen motivation to work for change. There is certainly a danger that a "back to the sixties" scenario would reverse recent trends and lead to declining energy and capability at the state and local level. Both voters and politicians in states and localities might decide to "let Washington do it."

Whatever its advantages or disadvantages, "back to the sixties" is unlikely to occur. It would take a major shift in people's willingness to pay taxes at the federal level. Given the current antagonism toward big government and lack of clarity about which level of government has responsibility for specific functions, this reversal of attitudes toward federal taxation is hard to imagine.

Dividing the Job

The third scenario is more realistic than "back to the sixties" and more workable than either of the other two. It is based on the premise that Washington has neither the managerial capacity nor the grass-roots support to simultaneously create a federal budget surplus, reform health financing, and implement the productivity agenda—while also managing increasingly demanding international responsibilities. It would be better to divide the job, focus the energies of the federal government on the parts of the task for which it has a distinct advantage, and rely on the states for activities they are more likely to carry out successfully.

"Dividing the job" would involve five major changes in policy. First, the federal government would take charge of reforming the nation's health financing system to accomplish two objectives: firm control of medical costs and universal health insurance. Cost control is crucial, since broadening coverage without controlling costs will only exacerbate medical inflation. Fees and remimbursement rates for all medical services would be set according to a negotiated formula that all providers would have to accept. Controlling the rate of increase of these fees and reimbursement rates would gradually reduce the rate of increase in medical spending to roughly the rate of growth of the economy as a whole. Universal coverage could be achieved by full national health insurance or, more likely, by some combination of private and public insurance. The new program would supplant medicaid, relieving state and local government of an increasing burden.

Even a limited public role would require additional federal revenues. Since these taxes, like current social security and medicare taxes, would be clearly related to identifiable benefits, they would be more acceptable to the electorate than general taxes to finance unspecified spending or deficit reduction. The health taxes should be earmarked for health services and deposited in a health insurance trust fund that would take over the spending functions now financed by medicaid and other health programs for low-income people. The size of the tax increase required would depend on the type of health financing program chosen, but even a limited reform would shift public spending for health from state and local budgets to the federal one. With successful control of medical cost inflation, it would be possible to provide health insurance for the currently uninsured without increasing total government health spending above that currently projected for the end of the decade. (For a more detailed discussion of health financing options, see chapter 9.)

Second, the states, not the federal government, would take charge of accomplishing a "productivity agenda" of reforms designed to revitalize the economy and raise incomes. These reforms would address needs such as education and skills training, child care, housing, infrastructure, and economic development. Once clearly in charge, the states would compete vigorously with each other to improve services and attract business by offering high-quality education, infrastructure, and other services.

Third, the following federal programs would be devolved to the states or gradually wither away: elementary and secondary education, job training, economic and community development, housing, most highways and other transportation, social services, and some pollution control programs. Some specific programs where federal action is needed would be retained, even expanded; for example, higher education scholarships for low-income students and federal support for scientific research, including research on learning. A few transportation functions— especially air traffic control—would remain federal. Devolving these functions would reduce federal spending by at least $75 billion. Much more important, devolution would reduce future pressure on the federal deficit. Citizens and organizations concerned about better housing, training, and education would have to lobby in their state capitals, not Washington.

Fourth, the federal government would bring its budget from deficit into surplus (including social security). It would then be adding to national saving and reducing the federal debt held by the public. The federal deficit would be eliminated by a combination of devolving domestic programs to the states, imposing health insurance taxes and transferring medicaid spending to a health insurance trust fund, and reducing other federal spending (including defense) faster than currently projected. Interest costs would also decline. General federal taxes need not rise.

Fifth, the states, with the blessing or the assistance of the federal government, would strengthen their tax systems and increase revenue by adopting one or more common taxes (same base, same rate) and sharing the proceeds. Common shared taxes would reduce border concerns and could enhance the revenues of poorer states. One version is a uniform value-added tax (VAT), shared on a per capita basis and substituted for state retail sales taxes. Another is a single state corporate income tax, perhaps collected by the IRS along with the federal tax, and shared on a formula basis. Another one is a shared energy tax. (These possibilities are discussed in greater detail in chapter 8.)

Compared with "back to the sixties," "dividing the job" implies a smaller federal government and a larger state-local sector. Tax increases would be required under both scenarios, since the deficit is to be reduced and more services provided in both. In "back to the sixties" all the new revenue would be raised at the federal level. In "dividing the job" additional revenue would come from a combination of new federal taxes for health insurance and increased state and local taxes for the productivity agenda.

Despite its name, the "dividing the job" scenario does not involve a return to dual federalism. There are important areas in which cooperative federalism is necessary and desirable. One of those is environmental protection. Many hazards to the environment cross state lines and cannot be satisfactorily dealt with by states and localities acting alone. Others are of largely local concern.

Welfare for families with children (AFDC) also remains a shared state and federal responsibility in this scenario. Some would argue for making AFDC federal or at least for a basic federal program that the states could supplement. Joint responsibility, however, would give both levels of government incentives to try hard to reduce welfare dependency. To this end, the states should improve education, training, and child care for welfare mothers, and the federal government should adjust the income tax to increase the after-tax rewards for low-wage work.

THE RATIONALE FOR "DIVIDING THE JOB"

A major premise underlying "dividing the job" is that citizens are anxious to revive the American dream. They want to live in an economy that provides sustainable and widely shared growth in the standard of living. They are prepared to work hard and make sacrifices to that end if they see the connection between the effort and the result. People want high-quality public services—schools that teach modern skills, retraining opportunities for workers who lose jobs, efficient transportation, health care for those who need it—but they also want to know what happens to the taxes they pay and see some evidence close to home that public efforts make a difference.

Successful economic revitalization is hard to carry out or even to comprehend on a national scale. Many of those concerned about the lagging American economy have urged the federal government to adopt an explicit industrial policy. Proponents usually envision a huge federal bank with a board allocating funds to industries and areas. Such grandiose notions founder on closer examination, however, in part because of the sheer size and diversity of the economy. Few would trust the federal government to allocate funds wisely or nonpolitically to development projects or programs. Washington cannot mobilize the community support, business-labor cooperation, or coordination that successful development requires.

Governors and mayors, however, are closer to the scene. They have more ways to generate business, labor, and community support for development and put together an effective program to increase investment and jobs. The best chance of having a successful industrial policy in a country this size is to have a lot of communities, states, and regions competing with each other to improve their own economic prospects.

Several scholars of federalism have argued that states are currently better suited than the federal government to undertake the economic development policies needed to ensure successful American competition in a global economy. David R. Beam has pointed out that although Americans came to rely on Washington for economic policy leadership in the Great Depression, the federal government did not have the answers when the economy began faltering in the 1970s.[2] The "supply-side" tax cutting of the early 1980s left the federal government with a paralyzing deficit. A national industrial policy was rejected out of fear that federal government efforts to choose and foster industrial "winners," as the Japanese supposedly do, would result in the government handing out political favors at taxpayers' expense. Meanwhile,

2. David R. Beam, "Reinventing Federalism: State-Local Government Roles in the New Economic Order," paper prepared for the 1988 annual meeting of the American Political Science Association.

however, states moved aggressively to improve their own economies and revenue bases. They set up public investment and venture capital funds, fostered technology and innovation, and sent missions abroad to attract foreign investment and promote regional exports. The new state development efforts emphasized skill training, education reform, business-university partnerships, and better transportation, rather than tax concessions to business.

Beam concluded that states are likely to do a better job in the economic development role than the federal government and ventures this hypothesis:

Under conditions of global competition and rapid technological change, a large nation composed of multiple political and economic centers, each striving to secure its own economic advantage, will be better able to advance the welfare of its citizens than a large nation dominated by a single political and economic center.[3]

In an earlier study, Paul Peterson and his colleagues examined federal grant programs in an attempt to discriminate between types of programs for which intergovernmental cooperation was productive and those for which it was counterproductive or unnecessary.[4] They found that "development programs" (vocational education, hospital construction, community development) were enthusiastically supported by state and local officials and easy to administer cooperatively. The federal government allowed state and local officials substantial discretion in using the money, and all parties thought the relationships were working well. "Redistributive programs" (compensatory education, rent subsidies, health maintenance organizations, special education) were much more contentious. These programs were directed at special groups with little political clout and mandated new kinds of services. States and localities usually tried diverting the funds to more general purposes. Then federal officials tightened the guidelines. Cooperation took time and effort.

Peterson and his coauthors concluded that federal development programs were unnecessary, except in occasional cases

3. Beam, "Reinventing Federalism," p. 16.
4. Paul E. Peterson, Barry G. Rabe, and Kenneth K. Wong, *When Federalism Works* (Brookings, 1986).

where the benefits spilled across state borders in a major way. In general, these programs would be undertaken by states and localities and run in much the same way without federal prodding. The "redistributive programs," however, accomplished national purposes that states and localities were resisting and would not have addressed without persistent intervention from Washington. The authors urged refocusing federal domestic policy to emphasize redistribution while confining federal economic development efforts to a few special cases.

This analysis suggests a major worry about "dividing the job," often expressed by traditional liberals, that states will neglect the less fortunate, particularly by retreating from federal efforts to improve the life chances of poor children. The fear has some basis, but poor and minority young people will not be left out if states play an aggressive role in economic development. Improving education, skills, and opportunities for the future labor force necessarily involves concentrating on the futures of low-income and minority young people, because they will make up such a large part of that labor force. Indeed, effective action to improve the skills and job prospects of the poor, especially young people, seems more likely if it is seen as essential to community and state economic development than if it is seen as federally funded redistribution policy.

Moreover, "dividing the job" does not involve federal abandonment of the poor. Low-income people would benefit most from universal health insurance. Most uninsured workers are in low-wage jobs, and one of the barriers to leaving welfare is fear of losing medicaid without gaining employer-provided health insurance. The federal food stamp program and joint federal-state funding of AFDC would also remain.

TWO PREVIOUS ATTEMPTS TO SORT OUT RESPONSIBILITIES

The idea of reexamining federal and state responsibilities is, of course, not a new one. In the 1970s and 1980s, concern with the proliferation of grants and the confusion of state and local roles led two presidents to propose new ways of sorting out the jobs.

Nixon's New Federalism

The administration of President Nixon, at least until it was paralyzed by the Watergate scandal and the ensuing impeachment proceedings, put unusual emphasis on improving the efficiency and effectiveness of government. Nixon's first term (1969–73) was a high watermark for White House concern with evaluation of program results, experimentation with policy innovation, and serious discussion of alternative ways of structuring responsibilities—both within Washington and between the federal and state levels—to make government work more efficiently.

Nixon's conservative ideology led him to emphasize sorting out federal and state functions more clearly, a concept he called New Federalism. He espoused a stronger role for the federal government in income maintenance and health care, although neither his family assistance plan nor his health proposals ever passed Congress. He believed in returning decisionmaking power to the states by cutting the number of categorical grants and providing federal aid to the states with fewer strings. In addition to general revenue sharing, he proposed a series of consolidations of categorical grant programs called "special revenue sharing." One hundred and twenty-nine separate programs were to be grouped into six block grants that the states could use for broad purposes such as education, transportation, and law enforcement, with relatively little interference from Washington.

The block grants had little success in Congress. Lobbyists for existing categorical programs fought to preserve their separate identity. In the end, only two of the proposed block grants were enacted, both in somewhat altered form. The Comprehensive Employment and Training Act of 1973 pulled together various manpower training programs, most enacted in the 1960s, into a single grant. The community development block grant program, which subsumed model cities and other funds for urban renewal, was passed by Congress and signed by President Gerald Ford in 1974.

The Reagan Swap Proposal

President Reagan's first year was dominated by his dramatic budget proposals (see chapter 6). Then in his second State of the

Union address in 1982, Reagan announced another drastic set of proposals, a series of "swaps" designed to sort out federal and state roles more clearly and reduce the number of categorical grants. The swap proposals, ill timed and ill thought out, met with strenuous opposition, not only in Congress, but in some parts of the state and local community as well. One salient feature was federal assumption of the full costs of medicaid in exchange for devolution to the states of the AFDC and food stamp programs. Such an exchange would have reversed the 1970s trend toward greater federal responsibility for welfare programs, reflected in the growth of the federal food stamp program and the creation of supplemental security income for the elderly, blind, and disabled poor in 1974. Most governors could see only fiscal catastrophe in agreeing to take on the full costs of AFDC and food stamps, especially in the recession year of 1982. If they had focused on the rapid escalation of medicaid costs that was already beginning to strain their budgets and worsened later in the decade, they might have found Reagan's deal more attractive.

Another feature of the swap was federal devolution of a diverse set of forty-four programs (125 separate grants) to the states in return for phasing out a group of federal taxes (alcohol, tobacco, and telephone taxes, part of the federal gasoline tax, and a windfall profits tax on oil and gas sales). Revenues from the designated taxes were initially to be deposited in a trust fund for the states, but the taxes themselves were to be reduced gradually and eliminated by 1991. If the states wanted to replace the lost federal revenue, they would have to raise their own taxes. States and localities, already adversely affected by recession and reductions in federal grants, were not enthusiastic about the swaps. After considerable negotiation and attempted compromise, the idea died.

Since President Reagan's ideas about federal-state relations bore some similarity to President Nixon's, both came to be described by the Nixon term, New Federalism. Both emphasized decentralization and restoring decisionmaking authority to state and localities. However, the Nixon proposals, especially revenue sharing, involved increases in the amount of money flowing from the federal treasury to state and localities. Reagan's intention, by contrast, was to reduce domestic spending at all levels. Nixon's revenue sharing program was eliminated and other grants were reduced. Reagan believed that devolving responsibilities to the states, especially for social programs, would lead to less total government spending because state and local taxpayers would be less willing than federal ones to foot the bill. His expectations were not realized, however. The federal retreat energized state and local government and led to higher state and local taxes.

HOW "DIVIDING THE JOB" DIFFERS

"Dividing the job" differs from both the Nixon and Reagan proposals. Moreover, changing economic and political circumstances make fundamental restructuring of the federal-state relationship both more necessary and more feasible in the 1990s than it was in the 1970s and 1980s.

"Dividing the job" involves devolution of whole federal functions to the states. The Nixon proposals, by contrast, merely combined specific categorical programs into more general block grants and perpetuated joint federal-state responsibility for the function in question. The Reagan plan did devolve specific programs, but did not offer any clear division of responsibility between the two levels.

The Reagan package would have diminished states' financial resources and added to the pressure on states to reduce services. The Nixon plan was more attractive to the states because it included general revenue sharing. However, as state officials are all too aware, GRS proved a fleeting boon. My proposal for common shared taxes, discussed in chapter 8, promises a more permanent and secure footing for state financing.

Moreover, restructuring the federal-state relationship is more urgent in the 1990s than it was even a decade ago. The lagging economy must be revitalized and the federal deficit eliminated. "Dividing the job" is an attempt to improve the chances of attaining both objectives.

EIGHT   *Paying for Stronger States*

have argued that the states should have clear responsibility for a specific set of services, including education and other public investments needed to increase the productivity of the American economy. States are better able to experiment and adapt to the special needs and strengths of their areas. They are more apt to command citizen loyalty and participation than faraway Washington.

Anyone who advocates increased reliance on states to improve public services, however, must address the question: Where will the states get the money? State governments have been struggling to meet the rising cost of public programs and have often encountered strenuous public resistance to tax increases. Budgetary stress in state capitals reached crisis proportions in the recession of 1990–92, when a large number of states were forced to cut spending and raise taxes in the face of mounting deficits.

126

Even in good times, states face two obstacles in raising the revenue needed to provide high-quality public services. First, states have unequal resources, and the poorer ones would have trouble financing adequate services even if their tax rates were high. Second, states compete with each other. They are reluctant to let their taxes get out of line with those of other states, especially neighboring states, for fear of losing businesses, sales, or people across the state line.

A new proposal that I call "common shared taxes" could mitigate both problems. A simple example would be a common sales tax shared by all the states. The tax rate would be identical in each state and would apply to the same types of sales. No one would have an incentive to shop in another state in order to avoid the tax. If the revenue were divided on the basis of state population—each state receiving the same amount per resident—poorer states would get back somewhat more than their own collections, because their per capita sales are below average.

WHERE THE MONEY COMES FROM

In 1990 state and local revenue totaled $740 billion—about 14 percent of GNP.[1] About 18 percent of state and local revenue came from the federal government. Property, sales, and income taxes accounted for most of the rest (figure 8-1). State and local funding also comes from an astonishing variety of other sources, such as lotteries, parking meters, fishing licenses, liquor store profits, water sales, bridge tolls, and university tuition.

In recent years, both states and localities have strengthened and diversified their revenue systems. Historically, the property tax was the main source of revenue for local governments and contributed to state finance as well. Property taxes tend to be unpopular, especially with older people who often find their property tax bill rising while their income is fixed. Protests against property taxes broke out in the 1970s, especially in areas

1. (Excludes social insurance contributions.) Advisory Commission on Intergovernmental Relations, *Significant Features of Fiscal Federalism*, vol. 2: *Revenues and Expenditures* (Washington, 1991), p. 46. States differ so greatly in the way they share responsibilities and revenues with their local governments that it is usually more comprehensible to lump state and local revenues together, rather than to discuss states and localities separately.

FIGURE 8-1.   *Sources of State and Local Revenue, 1990*[a]

Percent

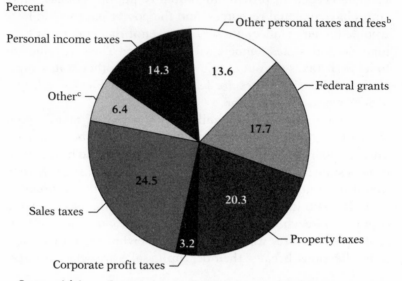

Source: Advisory Commission on Intergovernmental Relations, *Significant Features of Fiscal Federalism*, vol. 2: *Revenues and Expenditures* (Washington, 1991), p. 46.

a. Excludes contributions for social insurance.

b. Personal property taxes, estate and gift taxes, motor vehicle licenses, and personal nontaxes.

c. General and selected taxes, severance taxes, business licenses, and non-taxes.

where property values were rising more rapidly than income. In recent years, income taxes have become an increasingly important source of total state and local revenues, while the importance of property taxes has declined (figure 8-2). Both states and localities have also relied increasingly on fees and charges.

As states sought new tax sources and borrowed ideas from each other, their tax sources began to look more alike. In 1990 all but five states had general sales taxes. These apply to a wide range of goods and some services. Some states allow towns and cities to add a local sales tax. Most states also have excise taxes on selected items—notably alcohol, tobacco, and gasoline—as does the federal government. All but five states (and some localities) tax personal income. Enormous diversity remains, however, in rates and other specifics of state and local taxes.

FIGURE 8-2. *Major State and Local Taxes as a Percentage of Total Own-Source General Revenue, 1948–90*

Percent

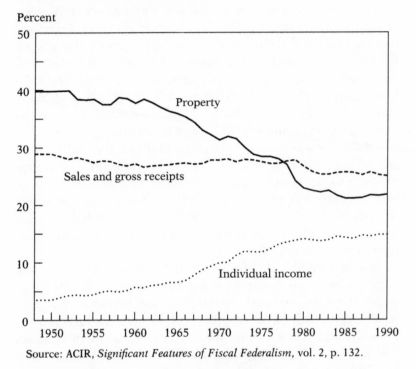

Source: ACIR, *Significant Features of Fiscal Federalism*, vol. 2, p. 132.

STATE AND LOCAL FISCAL STRESS

State and local governments ride a fiscal roller coaster. When the economy weakens—either nationally or regionally—income, sales, and property tax revenues shrink. At the same time, more unemployed and needy citizens seek state and local help. Unlike the federal government, state and local governments cannot normally borrow to cover operating expenses. In a recession, they must reduce services and lay off employees or increase tax rates, or both. When prosperity returns, however, state and local governments may find themselves suddenly flush. With leaner staffs and higher tax rates, they pile up surpluses that allow them to provide more services or reduce tax rates, or both—at least until the next recession hits.

This roller coaster pattern was evident in the 1980s. The "double dip" recession of 1980–82 was hard on most states and localities, especially since it coincided with "Reagan revolution" reductions in support from the federal government. States and localities drew down balances, cut services, laid off employees, and raised tax rates. In 1981–83, twenty-eight states increased income taxes and thirty states raised sales taxes.[2] Then, when the economy began growing again in 1983 and 1984, state and local finances improved. Indeed, surpluses at the state and local level partially offset the high federal deficits of the period. Many state and local governments were able to expand services and hire employees; some lowered tax rates again.

Recovery was most rapid in New England, the mid-Atlantic states, and California, however, where unemployment was low, property values soared, and government revenues increased rapidly. The farm belt and the "rust" belt, in contrast, were suffering from the high real interest rates and the overvalued dollar caused by huge federal deficits. Governmental finances in these areas continued to be strained.

In the second half of the 1980s, the good times for state and local governments began to peter out, except in the Midwest, where the economy finally began to revive. Aggregate state and local surpluses dropped substantially, despite the fact that the economy was still growing. When recession hit in 1990, states and localities staggered under the blow, in part because their fiscal condition had already weakened.

The deterioration in state and local fiscal health in the second half of the 1980s had several causes. Tax revenues grew more slowly than earlier in the decade because the economy was growing more slowly. Many governments, however, failed to face the reality of slower growth in tax revenues. Their expenditures continued to climb. In part, the growth in spending reflected the deteriorating economic situation of low-income families and neighborhoods. Homelessness, rising crime rates, escalating health costs, the AIDS epidemic, and the spreading drug crisis all put enormous upward pressure on state and local budgets, especially (but not exclusively) in cities.

2. Michael W. Larson and Karen M. Benker, *Significant Features of Fiscal Federalism* (Washington: Advisory Commission on Intergovernmental Relations, February 1986), table 53, p. 76.

FIGURE 8-3. *Federal Grants to States and Localities, Total and Individual Payments, Selected Years, 1960–90*

Percent of GNP

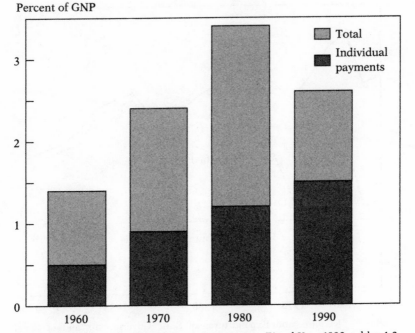

Source: *Budget of the United States Government, Fiscal Year 1992*, tables 1.2, 12.1.

Moreover, Washington was helping state and local governments less than in earlier years, and an increasing proportion of federal money was earmarked for welfare and medicaid, especially the latter (figure 8-3). Medicaid spending was escalating because the cost of medical care was rising rapidly, the number of needy young families eligible for medicaid was growing, and more elderly people with disabilities were turning to medicaid to pay for nursing home care. Congress, responding to growing public concern, mandated broader coverage and more services under medicaid, especially for children and pregnant women. Indeed, the rising cost of medicaid explains a large part of the deterioration in state and local fiscal health in the last half of the 1980s.[3]

3. Edward M. Gramlich, "The 1991 State and Local Fiscal Crisis," *Brookings Papers on Economic Activity, 1992:2*, pp. 249–75.

FIGURE 8-4.   *State and Local Budget Balances, 1970–90*

Percent of GNP

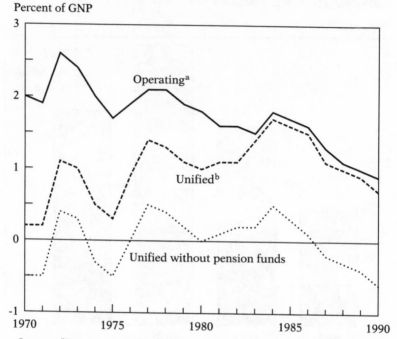

Source: "Receipts and Expenditures of State Governments and of Local Governments: Revised and Updated Estimates, 1959–84," *Survey of Current Business*, vol. 66 (May 1986), pp. 26–33; vol. 67 (November 1987), pp. 29–35; vol. 68 (September 1988), pp. 23–35; vol. 71 (July 1991), table 3.3, p. 10.
  a. Unified budget excluding pension funds and construction.
  b. State and local surplus and deficit.

  That deterioration can be clearly seen in figure 8-4, which shows the surpluses or deficits in budgets that include everything state and local governments do and the same surpluses and deficits if pension funds for state and local employees are excluded. Since the pension funds have been running surpluses (adding to the reserves needed to pay future benefits), subtracting them makes the state and local fiscal situation look worse. Most state and local borrowing, however, is done to finance capital projects, such as roads, not operating expenses. Subtracting construction spending gives a measure of the aggregate operating budget of state and local governments, which has remained in the black even in recession years. The three lines in figure 8-4 leave no doubt that, measured any way, the fiscal situation of states and localities was worsening in the mid-1980s, well before the 1990–92 recession.

The impact of the recession was most severe in the areas that enjoyed the most prosperity in the mid-1980s—California, New England, and the mid-Atlantic states. Governments in these areas, at both the state and local level, found their tax revenues falling and needs for services rising simultaneously. Facing huge potential deficits, even possible bankruptcy, they cut government payrolls and increased taxes. In the Midwest, where the recession was less severe and public spending had been restrained by earlier austerity, the government budget crunch was not so acute.

If the economic conditions of the last half of the 1980s— slow economic growth, increasing income inequality, escalating medical costs—continue in the 1990s, the outlook for state and local government budgets is disheartening. The federal government, with its huge deficit, is unlikely to provide significant financial help. Washington will continue to share the escalating cost of medicaid, but the medicaid burden on state and local government will also continue to rise. Additional mandates from the federal government without the funding to pay for them could make the state and local fiscal situation even grimmer.

If states and localities are to take on increased responsibilities for reviving the American economy, as I have argued they should, they will have to have more resources. However, there are two reasons why it may be especially difficult for states to raise revenues sufficiently to finance new levels of expenditure: they have unequal resources, and they are in competition with each other.

UNEQUAL STATE RESOURCES

Some states are a lot better off than others. States with relatively low per capita income, sales, and property values would have to tax their citizens at high rates to provide the same level of services that more fortunate states can provide with less tax effort.

Measuring State Inequality

In 1988 personal per capita income in Connecticut was 140 percent of the national average, while in Mississippi it was only 67 percent. At first glance, the capacity of taxpayers to finance public services appears to be twice as high in Connecticut as in Mississippi.[4]

Personal per capita income is not an ideal indicator of state capability to raise revenue, however, because some states have significant opportunities to raise revenue from residents of other states. States with outstanding tourist attractions can tax hotel and motel rooms, restaurant meals, and amusements that are used primarily by out-of-state residents. States with oil, gas, or mineral deposits can charge severance taxes that are paid primarily by purchasers outside the state. An alternative measure of tax capacity, known as the representative revenue system, reflects the range of revenue sources actually available to states and their localities.[5] On this index, some states rank higher than they do on personal income: Nevada, with its gambling casinos and show business; Delaware, where many national companies are incorporated; and Louisiana, Texas, and Oklahoma, especially in years of high oil prices. States without this special ability to "export" taxes, of course, rank lower than they would on personal income alone.

It costs more to deliver the same public services in some states than in others. For example, teachers' salaries, land values, and construction costs are higher in urban than in rural states. Some states also have problems that are more costly to deal with than those of other states (more poor children in school or more lane-miles of highways to repair, for example). Measures of fiscal capacity adjusted for the difficulties of problems faced are rough, but appear to show even bigger differences between poor and rich states than unadjusted measures of fiscal capacity.[6]

In sum, however they are measured, disparities among

4. *Survey of Current Business*, vol. 69 (August 1989), p. 34.
5. Advisory Commission on Intergovernmental Relations, *State Fiscal Capacity and Effort* (Washington, August 1990).
6. Robert W. Rafuse, Jr., "A Walk on the Expenditure Side: 'Needs' and Fiscal Capacity," *Intergovernmental Perspective*, vol. 16 (Fall 1990), pp. 25–30.

states are large. Some states fall consistently above or below the national average on any measure of fiscal strength.

One would expect regions of the country to become more alike in their economic levels over long periods as people and companies moved around in search of economic opportunities. In fact, disparities in average income among states appear to have diminished considerably since the nineteenth century.[7] Over the period from 1890 to 1988, states that originally had low incomes (especially in the South) grew faster than the national average, and many states that had high incomes at the end of the nineteenth century grew relatively slowly in the twentieth century. The pattern is uneven, however, and the convergence of earlier years has not been noticeable in recent decades.

Mitigating Inequality

Some parts of any country are likely to be more prosperous than others, so most countries face the question of how to reduce the inequality in public services among regional governments. Some approach the problem on the revenue side of the budget, collecting some taxes jointly or centrally and sharing the proceeds according to a formula that augments the revenues of the least affluent regions.

In the United States, however, the problem of mitigating inequalities among the states has been handled entirely on the spending side of the budget.[8] The federal government has reduced the significance of unequal state resources in two ways: by taking full national responsibility for some programs (such as social security) and by giving grants to the states for specific kinds of spending on a redistributive basis.

For example, highway grants from the federal government make possible better road systems than poor states could afford on their own. The interstate highway system has been a dramatic

---

7. Robert J. Barro and Xavier Sala-i-Martin, "Economic Growth and Convergence across the United States," Working Paper No. 3419 (Cambridge, Mass.: National Bureau of Economic Research, August 1990); and Barro and Sala-i-Martin, "Convergence Across States and Regions," *Brookings Papers on Economic Activity 1991:1*, pp. 107–82.

8. Tax sharing is sometimes used within states to mitigate inequalities among local jurisdictions.

example of this redistribution because the federal government put up 90 percent of the money. Even quite poor states could afford interstate highways when they were required to put up only 10 percent of the funds.

Some grants, such as those for public housing, Head Start, or compensatory education for low-income children, have been specifically designed to help low-income people. In some instances, such as medicaid or AFDC, the formula for distributing grants explicitly favors poorer states. The federal government pays a higher share of the funds in those states.

The principal of using federal spending programs to accomplish redistribution across state lines is an accepted feature of American federalism. Usually these programs have combined the two objectives of improving services and equalizing them. Under chapter 1 of the Elementary and Secondary Education Act, for example, the federal government simultaneously directs resources toward poor children and imposes rules about the type of compensatory education they are to receive. The only exception was the general revenue sharing (GRS) program enacted in the early 1970s. GRS gave both states and localities virtually unrestricted grants on the basis of a formula that favored poorer states. This exception, however, did not last long. When pressure mounted to reduce the federal deficit in the 1980s, GRS was abolished (see chapter 6).

With respect to revenues, by contrast, dual federalism lives on. The states and the federal government levy taxes independently within their own jurisdictions. They do not share revenues or redistribute them in any way. Some states model their income taxes on the federal one, but not even the District of Columbia has taken advantage of a federal offer to collect income tax on the states' behalf (a so-called piggyback tax).

One result is an enormously complex and overlapping tax system. The federal government taxes both individual and corporate income, as do most states. The federal government imposes excise taxes on gasoline, cigarettes, and alcoholic beverages, as do most of the states, although thus far there is no general federal sales tax.

Businesses that operate in more than one state find their activities considerably complicated by having to deal with so many tax codes. They employ tax experts to deal with multiple filings and to minimize tax liability. Difficult questions of how to allocate income or sales in a multistate operation have generated a large legal literature and considerable litigation, as well as some efforts by the states to agree on uniform standards and definitions.

The complexity of multiple tax systems, plus the inequality of revenues for public services in different states, suggests that the states ought to consider the possibility of imposing some common taxes and sharing the proceeds in a way that reduces inequality. The intense competition among states provides another argument for such a proposal.

INTERSTATE COMPETITION

When states consider tax increases, the question of what other states do looms large. If a state is considering increasing its sales tax, merchants in that state often express fear that consumers will make their purchases in another state to avoid the tax. The problem is of special concern where metropolitan areas straddle state lines—as do Philadelphia, Kansas City, St. Louis, and Washington, D.C., among others.

If the debate is about raising business taxes, enterprises may threaten to move to another jurisdiction, taking jobs and suppliers' markets with them. Indeed, states often seek to attract new companies by offering substantial business tax relief to firms considering a move.

If the proposal is to raise income taxes, politicians fear that affluent residents will move out in response to a rate increase, especially one that affects upper-income people. The state of Florida cannot enact an income tax without amending its constitution. Its politicians fear that an income tax would slow the stream of affluent people who retire to Florida and would cause political backlash among those who moved there in part to avoid paying state income tax.

Not all of the fears about tax-induced flight are well founded. Neither families nor businesses change their locations without cost and disruption. Taxes are rarely high on a list of reasons for moving. Businesses or individuals opposing a tax increase often exaggerate the likelihood that they will actually depart if the increase occurs.

Well founded or not, fear of losing people and businesses over the border frequently keeps state politicians from increasing taxes. Moreover, many states and localities, especially in the South, have engaged in competitive bidding to induce factories and other businesses to locate in their jurisdiction by offering tax concessions.

There are at least three reasons to believe that tax competitiveness among jurisdictions is becoming increasingly intense and will continue to do so. First, improvements in transportation and communications have greatly increased the mobility of people, goods, and services. Individuals change residences more frequently. They retire more often to locations far from their workplace and go longer distances to shop and vacation. At the same time, technology has made it easier for consumers and businesses to make purchases in distant places. They can use mail, telephone, fax machines, computers, and television to order goods and pay with nationally used credit cards. Catalog sales are growing rapidly, and shopping by interactive video hookup is likely to accelerate. Buyers have widening choices and increasing ability to find the most favorable prices and taxes.

Second, the economy is increasingly dominated by large national and international companies that operate in multiple locations. These companies can move their activities and the jobs that go with them around the country or even overseas in response to changing costs, including taxes. The accountants and tax lawyers of multistate and international firms are adept at attributing income to locations with low tax rates. On the other hand, dealing with disparate, and sometimes conflicting or overlapping, tax rules is complex and costly. Companies not only have to file a great many tax forms; they also incur litigation and lobbying costs in multiple jurisdictions. Multistate firms are beginning to realize that they would benefit from increased uniformity in state (and even international) tax laws.

Third, the ratio of goods to services in the economy has shifted dramatically toward services. Many kinds of services can be performed at a considerable distance from the client. Legal, accounting, financial, data processing, and many other services are frequently located far from the purchaser. Moreover, service establishments are usually easier to relocate than manufacturing plants with their heavy equipment and specialized facilities. Recent efforts of several states to include more services in the sales tax base illustrate these dilemmas.

CASUALTIES OF GO-IT-ALONE TAXATION

States under fiscal pressure have been seeking new revenues. Those that rely heavily on sales taxes have looked for types of sales that escape taxation, since broadening the base to which the tax applies brings in more revenue without imposing higher rates.

Catalog sales are an obvious example of cross-border transactions that escape state taxation. Such sales have been growing rapidly, and states would like to tax them along with other retail sales. In-state retailers resent competition from untaxed out-of-state mail order operations. In 1967 the Supreme Court ruled that a state cannot tax the sale of items ordered from the catalog of a merchant in another state unless the merchant has a physical presence in the taxing state.[9] The Court was concerned in part that requiring catalog firms to collect sales taxes and remit them to multiple state and local jurisdictions would impose an excessive burden on these firms. States persisted, however, and the Court agreed to hear another case on this issue in its 1991–92 term.

Of far greater importance to state revenues than catalog sales is the rapid growth in sales of services. Since a growing portion of consumer spending goes for services rather than for goods, states have been eager to extend their retail sales taxes to services. Attempts to do do, however have met with obstacles related to the mobility of services across state lines, as illustrated by recent episodes in Florida and Massachusetts.

The Florida Experience

In 1987, the state of Florida faced an urgent need for additional revenue. Expenses were rising, and tax revenues were not

9. *National Bellas Hess* v. *Illinois Department of Revenue*, 386 U.S. 753 (1967).

keeping up. Since property taxes are devoted to local governments, and the state constitution prohibits a personal income
tax, the state government depends almost entirely on two
sources, the corporate income tax and the sales tax. The sales
tax, which produced about two-thirds of the state's revenue in
1987, excluded services, except for those used primarily by tourists, such as hotels, motels, and amusements. (Taxing out-of-
state visitors is usually popular with states' residents.)

The service economy in Florida has been expanding, while
sales of goods have not kept up with rising income. If the state
was to increase revenue, it had two choices: raise the rate on
items currently taxed or include more services. Proponents of
taxing services argued that people who chose to buy services
instead of goods should not escape the sales tax. Moreover, since
people buy more services as their income rises, the tax on services
was likely to be less regressive than a tax on goods. Some opponents pointed out that many services (law, accounting, advertising, construction) are purchased by companies that produce
goods or other services. If the sales tax is applied both to the
services a business buys and to its output, the services are sub-
jected to more than one tax—a phenomenon known as tax pyramiding. Proponents countered that retail sales taxes are also
collected on some goods that are sold to businesses, so pyramiding is not special to services.

After considerable controversy, a law was drafted that extended the sales tax to many professional and personal services,
including law, accounting, data processing, construction, and
advertising. Medical, social, and educational services were exempt.

The designers of the services tax had to decide how to treat
residents who buy something in another state to use at home.
Florida, like other states with sales taxes, has a "use tax." A
Florida resident who buys a car in another state pays a use tax
when registering it in Florida, rather than a sales tax to the state
in which he bought it. Since most purchases are not registered,
however, use taxes are hard to enforce. Consumers rarely call up
the state government and say, "I just bought a new stereo system
in another state; where do I send the check for the use tax?"

The Florida legislation imposed a use tax on services used
in Florida but purchased elsewhere. For example, the purchaser

of advertising in a national magazine would be liable for tax on a percentage of the advertising fee equal to the Florida share of the total circulation of the magazine.

The debate over the service tax extension was heated. Opponents claimed that Florida businesses would lose their competitive position because their services would cost more and that Florida would become a less attractive place to do business. Other opponents criticized the administrative complexity and paperwork involved in collecting the tax, especially the provisions designed to enforce the use tax.

The sales tax extension was enacted, but the matter did not end there. National advertisers led a barrage of opposition to the new law. Trade associations boycotted Florida as a meeting site. Within a few months, the governor and the legislature repealed the tax on services and raised the rate on the existing base instead.

Massachusetts and Other States

In the fall of 1990, Massachusetts enacted a broad-based tax on services. The state was also facing a large budget deficit, and service industries, a growing part of the Massachusetts economy, were mostly exempt from sales taxation. The governor and the legislature, reluctant to raise either sales or income tax rates before an election, extended the sales tax to most services.

The Massachusetts law exempted advertising services, in part because lawmakers feared a national advertising onslaught like the one that overturned the Florida law. The bill that passed the Massachusetts Senate included financial services, but heavy lobbying, especially by mutual funds, was successful in excluding financial services from the final legislation.

Many of the arguments against the tax involved border questions. It was alleged that Massachusetts would handicap its service industries and that they would leave the state. As Richard A. Manley, president of the Massachusetts Taxpayers Foundation, put it, "Massachusetts is the birthplace of the mutual fund industry. I think you'll lose them all. It's one thing for a manufacturing company to move. For a lot of these folks it's a matter of putting a computer on a truck and getting out."[10] The services

10. Joseph Pereira, "Massachusetts Considers Broad Sales Tax on Services in the Bid to Close Budget Gap," *Wall Street Journal*, May 30, 1990, p. A2.

tax became an issue in the gubernatorial campaign of 1990. Shortly after his inauguration, the new governor, William Weld, convinced the legislature to repeal the tax.

Most states with sales taxes are experiencing similar pressure to extend the tax to services. Some have begun including selected services. For example, Connecticut, New York, Illinois, and the District of Columbia have considered extending their sales taxes to the legal, accounting, and advertising industries, but have backed down in the face of concerted lobbying and fears of a service exodus. The few states that do have broad-based service taxes (such as Hawaii, South Dakota, and New Mexico) do not have big service industries likely to relocate somewhere else. To obtain major revenues from service industries, states may have to act jointly.

COMMON SHARED TAXES: A NEW APPROACH

States might provide higher-quality services if they shared some taxes and did not have to worry so much about losing businesses to neighboring states with lower tax rates. They would then have more incentives to compete on the basis of the excellence of their services. They would have to attract businesses and residents with good schools, parks, and transportation, rather than with tax breaks. The common taxes would also simplify the tax structure and lower the compliance costs facing companies that operate in many states, as well as reducing the enforcement costs of the tax collectors. Joint action, of course, might not look so attractive to the taxpayer who could no longer escape across the border to a low-tax state.

Sharing a Retail Sales Tax

All but five states tax sales at the retail level.[11] Rates differ substantially, however, and so do the list of goods and services to which the taxes apply. Many states exempt food, for example. Only a few tax medicines. Most apply the tax to only a limited list of services.

11. The exceptions in 1991 were: Alaska, Delaware, Montana, New Hampshire, and Oregon. Advisory Commission on Intergovernmental Relations, *Significant Features of Fiscal Federalism*, vol. 1: *Budget Processes and Tax Systems* (Washington, 1991), table 29.

States could avoid border problems in retail sales taxation by agreeing to tax a common set of goods and services at the same rates and to divide the proceeds according to a formula. The idea might be especially attractive to a group of contiguous states (such as New England, or the southern or Pacific Northwest states). If all fifty states joined an interstate compact to share the proceeds of a uniform sales tax, the result would be a national (but not federal) tax on goods and services.

Alternatively, Congress could pass a general sales tax and share it with the states to compensate them for federal preemption of one of their traditional revenue sources. Another version of this idea would be a federal sales tax on which the states could piggyback, adding their own sales taxes to the federal one if they chose to do so. The federal government would collect both taxes and remit the state portion to the states. Since the federal government has no experience in collecting general sales taxes and no special advantage in doing so, it has been suggested that the states keep their own sales taxes but collect an additional percentage on behalf of the federal government and remit these funds to Washington—an arrangement that might be called "reverse revenue sharing."[12] These piggyback arrangements would not result in uniform taxation, but would probably reduce the disparity among states considerably.

The retail sales tax is familiar to American taxpayers and tax collectors, but it is not necessarily the best instrument for taxing sales. Many other countries, including all the members of the European Economic Community, use a sales tax called a value-added tax (VAT), which has some superior features. If the states break with the go-it-alone tradition and join in a common sales tax, they should consider substituting a common VAT for their retail sales taxes.

A Common Shared Value-Added Tax

A retail sales tax is supposed to tax sales to final consumers, not to producers or wholesalers. However, sales are frequently taxed at intermediate stages. For example, the government may

12. John A. Miller, "State Administration of a National Sales Tax: A New Opportunity for Cooperative Federalism," *Virginia Tax Review*, vol. 9 (Fall 1989), pp. 243–71.

collect tax on the materials used by an electrician and again on his bill to a client. In this case, the government is taxing a tax. The value-added tax is a sales tax explicitly designed to avoid double counting. A product or service is taxed at each stage of its production, but the tax falls only on the value added at that stage.

There are many ways to structure a VAT. Under one method, sellers pay a tax on total sales minus materials and services purchased from other businesses. Alternatively, sellers can calculate the tax on total sales and deduct the tax that has been paid at previous stages by their suppliers. The latter method has some self-enforcing features. Retail sellers, for example, will want to minimize their tax by making sure that they get proof of the tax payment from their wholesalers.

In the United States, the value-added tax has not been a part of the tax tradition, except in Michigan. Michigan's "single business tax," adopted in place of a retail sales tax and other business taxes, is a form of value-added tax. Other states rely on retail sales taxes.

In recent years, a federal VAT has frequently been proposed as a solution to the federal deficit problem. Proponents of a federal VAT argue that if more revenues are needed to pay for federal services, a nation so short of saving should increase its taxes on consumption rather than income. Moreover, a VAT can be rebated to exporters and hence does not penalize U.S. competitiveness in international trade.

Proposals for a federal VAT have not received serious political consideration, however, for at least three reasons. First, state and local governments view federal entry into general sales taxation as a threat to their long-run ability to raise revenue. Hence they oppose both a VAT and a retail sales tax at the federal level.

Second, a VAT, like a retail sales tax, is regressive. If the budget deficit were reduced by imposing a federal VAT, the burden would fall more heavily on low- and middle-income people than it would if the same amount of revenue were raised from an income tax surcharge.[13]

Third, since the federal government does not have a general

---

13. Congressional Budget Office, *Effects of Adopting a Value-Added Tax* (February 1992), p. 35.

sales tax, it would have to enact a whole new structure to collect a VAT. Collection costs could be significant.

A common shared VAT at the state level, however, would enhance, not threaten, state and local fiscal health. If a shared VAT were substituted for current state retail sales taxes, states would benefit from the additional revenue collected on cross-border sales now escaping taxation. They would be able to extend their sales taxes to services with less concern about either double counting or migration of service providers to other states. The VAT need be no more regressive than existing state sales taxes and could be less so, since higher-income people devote more of their incomes to services. Incremental collection costs would also be lower at the state level, since most states already collect sales taxes. Hence a VAT is a strong candidate for a common tax to be shared by the states.

A Common Shared Corporate Income Tax

The federal government taxes corporate income, as do most states. Because state corporate income taxes differ widely in rate and definition of income, multistate corporations have to file different tax returns in each state in which they operate. Corporate tax accountants try to find ways of allocating the corporation's total income in a way that minimizes the tax paid. States, for their part, try to get as much as possible. Corporations allege that they are paying tax on the same income in more than one jurisdiction. The evidence, however, indicates that some corporate income escapes any taxation at the state level.[14]

A common shared corporate income tax would reduce compliance and enforcement costs and tax corporate income fairly— and only once. The common shared state tax could be separate from the federal corporate income tax or combined with it. A single national tax shared by the federal government with the states (the German model) has some appeal.

A Common Shared Gasoline Tax

The federal government and most states tax gasoline, and many states worry about their gasoline taxes getting out of line

14. Robert P. Strauss, "Considerations in the Federal Collection of State Corporate Income Taxes," *State Tax Notes*, September 16, 1991, pp. 81–89.

with their neighbors' taxes. When a state is small, or has concentrations of population on the borders, motorists may fill up in a neighboring state with lower gas taxes. When a major interstate highway goes through the corner of a state, truckers may take advantage of tax differences.

Gasoline taxes have traditionally been used to finance highways, because gasoline use was considered a rough approximation of highway use.[15] In recent years, however, a substantial increase in gasoline taxes—far above the level that could be used for highways plus mass transit—has been proposed as a contribution to energy conservation and pollution reduction.

The United States uses gasoline much more profligately than other countries, because it is cheap here. The United States used to produce most of its own oil and had little incentive to conserve it. A relatively low gasoline tax produced enough revenue for roads because Americans drove a great deal and liked big cars. Countries that were more dependent on imported oil taxed gasoline heavily and provided incentives to the production and purchase of smaller, more fuel-efficient vehicles.

Now the United States is running out of domestic oil that can be produced cheaply and is increasingly dependent on imported oil. In the 1970s, when OPEC restricted oil exports, Americans learned suddenly how much their lives could be disrupted by foreign suppliers of oil.

Substantial increases in gasoline taxes would promote fuel efficiency and reduce dependence on imported oil. Motorists would have strong incentives to buy more fuel-efficient cars and to switch to public transportation. Automakers would have incentives to invest in new technology for improving fuel efficiency. Governments would have revenue, not only for better roads, but also for other public purposes.

The automobile is also a major contributor to poor air quality, especially in metropolitan areas with inadequate public

15. In fact, gasoline use is a poor measure of wear and tear on the roads (which depends mainly on vehicle weight per axle), or of the congestion costs imposed on others by a vehicle's use of the road at peak hours. Shifting to congestion-related tolls and truck taxes based on weight would improve the efficiency of highway construction and use. Kenneth A. Small, Clifford Winston, and Carol A. Evans, *Road Work: A New Highway Pricing and Investment Policy* (Brookings, 1989), p. 7.

transportation, such as Los Angeles. Automobile emissions are not only unpleasant and unhealthy, but also contribute to the accumulation of greenhouse gases in the atmosphere.

Gas tax increases should be phased in slowly to avoid hardship. A gradual increase announced in advance would allow people to adjust their life-style, automobile producers and other companies to improve their technology, and governments to develop new transportation networks.[16]

Fierce opposition to even small increases in the gas tax reveals the psychological importance of the automobile in American life. Opponents argue that the gasoline tax is regressive, meaning that it takes a greater proportion of the income of the poor than of the middle class. There is no strong evidence to support this position. General sales taxes are probably more regressive than gasoline taxes but are far less unpopular. States also fear that increased gasoline taxes at the federal level will increase resistance to state tax increases. A common shared tax on gasoline at the state level would be a different matter. It would be particularly plausible if responsibility for highways and mass transit were devolved to the states.

A gasoline tax is estimated to raise almost $1 billion per penny of tax. Hence an increase of 20 cents a year for five years would ultimately raise nearly $100 billion, or substantially more than would be needed for highways.[17] The additional revenue should be used for education, skills training, or economic development.

MAKING THE DECISIONS

Implementing a common shared tax requires some mechanism for deciding the initial rate and the base of the tax (for example, 6 percent on retail sales except food and medicine); by whom the tax is to be collected; by what formula the revenues

16. The argument is sometimes made that increasing the gasoline tax would put the United States at a competitive disadvantage vis-à-vis other industrial countries. Our principal competitors, however, have much higher gasoline taxes than we do.

17. Congressional Budget Office, *Reducing the Deficit: Spending and Revenue Options* (February 1992), p. 340. To the extent that the higher tax induced energy conservation, the revenue yield would be reduced.

are to be divided; and how future changes in the rate or the base of the distribution formula are to be arrived at.

One possibility is for the federal government to enact the tax and distribute it to the states. Another is for the states—groups of contiguous states or all fifty—to work out the problems themselves by interstate compact. Still another is a federal tax credit for uniform state taxes. All approaches would have advantages and disadvantages.

Federal Enactment

The most straightforward and practical way to implement a common shared tax would be for Congress to enact a federal law levying a national tax on behalf of the states and specifying a formula for distributing it among them. The law could specify that the revenues collected were to be allocated entirely to the states and were not available for any federal purpose. The funds could be run through an off-budget trust fund and need not appear in the federal budget.

Deciding on the nature of the tax to be shared, defining the base, and setting the rate and the distribution formula would involve negotiations among the administration, the tax-writing committees of Congress, and the states. Organizations such as the National Governors' Association, the National Conference of State Legislatures, the Council of State Governments, the MultiState Tax Commission, and the Advisory Commission on Intergovernmental Relations would presumably be involved in working out the details.

One advantage of the federal legislation route would be the familiarity of the federal tax-writing process. The federal government could enact a national tax for the states without obtaining the agreement of all fifty states, although the political impetus would clearly have to come primarily from the state level. Without strong, nearly universal support from the states, Congress would be unlikely to act.

The disadvantage of the federal route is that Congress would be tempted to attach conditions, either at the time of enactment of the common shared tax or later. Given the history of revenue sharing, state officials are understandably skeptical about the good faith of the federal government in establishing a permanent fund for states. The federal route would be acceptable to the states only with strong safeguards against federal interference. Drastic as such a suggestion might seem, enshrining the common shared tax fund in a constitutional amendment might be necessary to ensure its survival and immunity from congressional tinkering.

An Interstate Compact

Alternatively, states could negotiate an interstate compact to levy and share a common tax. Interstate compacts require the approval of the federal government, but except for giving its formal blessing the federal government need not be involved, either in the decisions or in the implementation of the compact.

An interstate compact establishing a common shared tax would be complicated. The compact would have to describe the tax to be levied, define the base, and set the initial tax rate or schedule of rates. It would have to define a formula for dividing the revenues and set up a mechanism for collecting the tax and distributing the proceeds. It would also have to define procedures for repealing or altering the initial agreement. For example, all states that were parties to the compact could agree to adopt any change ratified by three-quarters of the states.

The interstate compact approach would dramatize the fact that the common shared tax is a state tax, not a federal one. The federal government would not have an easy way of imposing conditions on how the money was spent, nor could Congress simply repeal the tax as it did with revenue sharing.

The interstate compact method is cumbersome, however. It would be nearly impossible to get all fifty states to agree to the same tax. The existence of even a few holdouts might cause other states to worry about losing sales or jobs to the nonparticipating states. For the states to come to an agreement on such a complicated and politically charged arrangement would take strong leadership by a substantial number of governors and a new level of cooperation among the states to solve their common fiscal problems.

Federal Tax Credits

Another approach would be for the federal government to use its tax power to encourage the states to enact common (but not shared) taxes. The federal government would enact a tax, say a VAT, but would give full credit to any taxpayer who paid an identical state tax. States would then have an overwhelming incentive to enact a VAT (presumably in place of their retail sales tax) in order to collect revenue that would otherwise go to the federal government. Thus congressional action would determine the nature and structure of the tax, but states that acted to take advantage of the federal credit would be able to use the money they collected without federal interference.[18]

This possibility is attractive because it is more familiar and less cumbersome than the interstate compact route but leaves decisions on how to spend the money in state hands. By itself, however, the tax credit approach would not involve redistribution of the revenues toward needier states.

A federal tax with a partial tax credit should also be considered. For example, the federal government could pass a 6 percent VAT and allow a credit for a state VAT of up to 5 percent. The additional 1 percent could be used for federal purposes or for supplementary grants to the neediest states. This approach could easily be applied to gasoline or other energy taxes. For example, the federal government could increase the gasoline tax by 20 cents a year for five years to encourage energy conservation and reduce air pollution. A tax credit could enable states to pick up half the revenue. States could then afford to take over highway and other programs now funded by the federal government. The federal government, in turn, could reduce the budget deficit substantially as a result of both devolving responsibilities to the states and acquiring additional revenues.

If the tax credit approach were combined with redistribution of revenues toward poorer states, the result would bear considerable resemblance to the federal-state sharing of taxes that occurs in Germany.

THE GERMAN APPROACH TO FISCAL FEDERALISM

In the German federal system, major revenue comes from shared taxes on income and sales.[19] A uniform individual income

18. The federal unemployment tax and the federal estate tax work in this fashion.
19. Annette Dengel, "The Tax System of the Federal Republic of Germany," Brookings Discussion Papers in Economics, April 1986. The discussion refers to fiscal federalism in West Germany, before unification.

tax, for example, is levied on all Germans and the proceeds are shared by three levels of government: a modest portion is reserved for local government and the balance is shared equally by the federal government and the *Länder*. Similarly, a uniform corporate income tax is paid by all corporations doing business in Germany. The proceeds are divided equally between the federal government and the *Länder*.

The existence of uniform income taxes simplifies life for German taxpayers, both individual and corporate. Even a German taxpayer earning income in several *Länder* files just one income tax, while an American taxpayer normally files at least two—one at the federal level and one or more at the state level. For national corporations with operations in many parts of the country, the German system is less complex and costly than the American one.

The German shared income taxes do not redistribute revenue across borders. The *Länder*'s portion of the individual income tax, for example, is shared according to the domicile of the taxpayer. The main vehicle for equalization is the VAT. A single VAT is shared between the federal level and the *Länder* governments. The portion shared by the *Länder* is divided on the basis of population. This means that the wealthier areas that generate high per capita value added subsidize poorer ones that generate lower per capita value added. In addition, a portion of the federal government's share goes as a supplementary grant to financially weak *Länder*. The objective of this aggressive redistribution is to equalize fiscal resources available to governments in different parts of the country without impairing the budgetary autonomy of the *Länder* within their sphere of jurisdiction.

THE POLITICS OF COMMON SHARED TAXES

Interest in reducing the diversity of tax systems is growing around the world as economies become more interdependent and taxpayers move more easily across borders. The countries of the European Community are making their taxes more uniform as they eliminate trade barriers among themselves. The American states, by contrast, have never made serious efforts to harmonize their taxes, although they have been part of a common market for more than 200 years.

The most frequently voiced objection to the idea of common shared taxes in the United States is political infeasibility. Skeptics allege that Congress would not enact a major tax whose proceeds would be spent by other levels of government and that states do not have the tradition of cooperation that would permit them to form an interstate compact to share one or more common taxes. Even if they cooperated to the extent of putting a common tax into operation, the rich states would certainly want to retain all the revenue generated in their jurisdiction and not share it with less affluent states.

These objections may well be valid, but many policies initially labeled "politically infeasible" have eventually come to pass. The need for additional state revenue is great, even without devolution of federal functions, and states are increasingly conscious of the need to find a way of taxing growth sectors of the economy, especially services. They are also increasingly aware of the mobility of taxpayers and tax sources across borders in an increasingly interlinked national and global economy. Cooperation on common taxes might start in a small way—say with catalog sales or professional services—and then spread to a larger portion of the tax base. Acceptance of a formula for dividing revenues, such as by population, would have the appeal of simplicity, even if it involved some redistribution. Moreover, redistribution is easier to swallow if the whole revenue pie is growing, as it would be if common taxation allowed the states to tax sources that are now escaping taxation altogether by moving, or threatening to move, across borders.

It might also be possible to convert Congress to the idea of common shared taxes for the states—without federal strings—if the idea were part of a new and clearer division of responsibility between the federal government and the states as well as a solution to the federal deficit problem. Members of Congress and federal executives increasingly express a sense of frustration with the current federal role and an awareness of the extreme burden placed on Washington. Given the escalating challenges of global interdependence and the clear need to reinvigorate the economy, radical notions like devolution and common shared taxes might attract support.

NINE   *Social Insurance:*
A Federal Priority

The public actions needed to revitalize the American economy cannot be carried out by states and localities alone. In the scenario for "dividing the job," crucial roles are also assigned to Washington. The federal government must work with other countries to enhance mutual security, settle disputes peacefully, ensure the flow of trade and investment around the world, and preserve the global environment. It must undertake activities that the states are unlikely to support adequately on their own, such as funding scientific research and encouraging technological development. One of the most crucial roles for the federal government already dominates the federal budget: strengthening the nation's social insurance system.

In particular, the federal government is far better suited than the states for resolving the health cost crisis. It should take the lead in controlling the growth of health costs while ensuring universal access to health care. Washington should also strengthen the social security system and protect its reserves by balancing the rest of the federal budget.

THE CASE FOR SOCIAL INSURANCE

A strong social insurance system makes it possible for a private enterprise economy to function more productively. Private firms competing in free markets can generate high standards of living for consumers. In attempting to increase their own profits, private companies try to anticipate what consumers want, vie with each other to invent new products and services, and compete to lower the cost of producing and selling. The bureaucratized enterprises of centrally planned economies are both less efficient and less responsive to consumer desires than are competing private firms, as the collapse of the communist bloc economies amply demonstrates.

Centrally planned economies, however, provide lifetime security for workers, while market economies impose high costs on some people. To compete effectively, private firms must take risks, try new ideas, and be flexible enough to shift to new products, processes, and locations. Inevitably, some ventures fail. Workers are laid off. Families and communities suffer severe losses. A strong social insurance system reduces the impact of economic change and helps stabilize the economy so that the ups and downs of the business cycle are less devastating. If social insurance is inadequate, firms will be under much more pressure, internal and external, to avoid risk taking and restructuring that might cost jobs. The whole economy will function less productively.

The United States realized the need for social insurance when the economy collapsed in the 1930s, and it has been building and adjusting its system ever since. As the countries of the former communist bloc struggle with the challenge of shifting to a market system, they will have to create new social insurance systems to protect individuals from the hazards of the transition and of the new market system itself.

Some argue that social insurance is an unnecessarily expensive way to assist the relatively small number of people who fall through the cracks in a private enterprise system. They favor a "safety net" that catches only those who actually fall—means-tested programs for those who can prove they are destitute.

Means-tested programs, by definition, target funds toward those who need them most and hence reduce the amount of money the government must move around. For example, since social security takes in money from all workers and pays benefits to all retirees regardless of need, it must move massive amounts of money in and out of the federal treasury. If the government paid benefits out of general taxes only to elderly people who could prove they had inadequate incomes, the sums involved would be much smaller. Social security would no longer be a "middle-class entitlement" (it is really an every-class entitlement); it would be a welfare program for the elderly poor. Most people would have to rely on private pension plans and personal savings for their retirement income. Similarly, the medicare program, which provides health insurance for older people regardless of need, takes in and pays out more money than it would if it provided benefits only to the needy elderly.

Others, including the author, believe that social insurance is far superior to welfare precisely because it benefits the whole population, not just the needy. Social security, medicare, and other social insurance programs command broad public support. People regard these benefits as earned rights because they contributed out of their wages. No shame is attached to drawing a social security check or sending a hospital bill to medicare for reimbursement. Welfare and medicaid recipients, by contrast, are viewed as freeloaders by much of the taxpaying public, even when the circumstances that forced them to apply for benefits are not of their own making. When budgets are tight, welfare benefits and services to low-income people often get cut while social insurance usually does not. There is much truth to the saying "programs for the poor are poor programs." The standard of living of the elderly would almost certainly be lower and their medical care far less adequate if social security and medicare did not exist and they had to rely on private pensions, savings, and private insurance plus welfare and charity.

One of the most critical roles the federal government can play in reviving the American dream is to strengthen social insurance, so that the private sector can compete more vigorously and the need for welfare programs can gradually diminish. The most urgent need is to expand social insurance to include health care coverage for all Americans.

REFORMING HEALTH INSURANCE

The United States has a curious distinction among the industrial democracies: it is the only country without universal health insurance. Americans have long been ambivalent about whether health care should be regarded as a purely private responsibility or one in which the whole society has a stake. The nation's first social insurance programs protected individuals against loss of income from unemployment, disability, death of the breadwinner, and retirement. The risk of incurring health costs was left out until 1965, when the medicare program was enacted.

Medicare provides insurance for older and some disabled Americans against the costs of acute illness. Only part A, which covers hospital bills, is true social insurance. Like social security, it is funded by a tax on wages. Part B, which covers doctors' bills and outpatient services, is partially financed out of premiums paid by the elderly, but most of the money (about three-fourths in 1991) comes out of general taxes.[1] Hence the general taxpayer subsidizes part B benefits for the elderly regardless of need.

The nonelderly population, by contrast, has no social insurance for health care. Most obtain health insurance through their employers, but coverage varies enormously. Large firms tend to offer generous health benefits, while smaller ones are likely to offer more meager benefits or none at all. High-income workers are far more likely than low-income workers to have insurance provided by their employer.

People without insurance are dependent on their own resources or some kind of charity. Medicaid, which is a joint federal-state program, finances health care for welfare recipients and

1. *Overview of Entitlement Programs, 1991 Green Book, Background Material and Data on Programs within the Jurisdiction of the Committee on Ways and Means: 1991 Edition*, Committee Print, House Committee on Ways and Means, 102 Cong. 1 sess. (Government Printing Office, 1991), p. 173.

some other people who can prove financial need. Its benefits vary greatly from state to state.

Two Problems

In recent years, the fragmented system by which Americans pay for health care has come under increasing pressure and has generated mounting dissatisfaction. Two serious weaknesses are apparent. First, the system provides no effective controls on the cost of care. Spending for health care in the United States rose from about 7.3 percent of GNP in 1970 to 12.3 percent in 1990 (see figure 5-2). If current trends continue, Americans will devote about 17 percent of their entire output to health care by 2000. Canada, France, and Germany spend about three-quarters as much of their total output on health care as we do, and their health costs are rising less rapidly than ours. Nevertheless, their citizens generally get good health care and are at least as healthy as Americans.[2]

Second, there are huge gaps in coverage. About 33 million Americans, predominantly young adults and children, had no health insurance at all in 1989. Another 21 million were dependent on the medicaid program.[3] Many of those who do have insurance have only limited coverage. They would be bankrupted by serious illness. Moreover, only a tiny fraction of the population (even of the elderly population, who are most at risk) has insurance against the cost of long-term care, such as nursing home and home health care. Medicare covers acute illness, not chronic conditions and disabilities that may require long-term care.

The two problems—rising cost and inadequate coverage—aggravate each other. As the cost of care has risen, health insurance premiums have escalated. Insurance companies have offered more favorable premiums to large companies, especially those that have young and healthy employees who do not perform hazardous work. They have also tried to keep premiums down by excluding people with known health problems. The

2. General Accounting Office, *Health Care Spending Control: The Experience of France, Germany, and Japan,* HRD-92-9 (September 1991), p. 19.
3. *Overview of Entitlement Programs,* Committee Print, pp. 307, 1410.

result has been higher premiums (or no coverage at all) for those not in the favored groups. Many small businesses, facing higher health insurance premiums and higher administrative costs than big businesses, have dropped health benefits. Low-wage workers, and those in hazardous occupations, have been especially hard hit. As more and more people have found themselves unprotected or dependent on welfare or charity, fear has spread, even among the well-insured, that their coverage is in jeopardy. The cost of medicaid and other public programs for those without private insurance has risen rapidly and become a growing burden for taxpayers at all levels.

If Americans were buying higher-quality care and living longer, healthier lives than citizens of other industrial countries, their higher level of health care spending would be justified. Evidence suggests, however, that much of the excess spending in the United States reflects inefficiency, redundancy, and administrative costs that do not improve health. If the United States continues to spend an increasing share of its national output on health care (without evident payoff in health results) while other industrial countries spend much less, the American standard of living will fall progressively behind theirs even if U.S. output keeps up. Moreover, continuously escalating medical costs will increase the proportion of the population without adequate insurance and intensify the rising inequality in the American standard of living. Hence controlling health costs should have high priority in any plan to revitalize the American economy.

Controlling Medical Costs

When most health bills are paid by a third party—either an insurance company or a government program—neither the patient nor the health service provider has much incentive to hold down the cost of care. At the time of treatment both the patient and the doctor or hospital have an interest in the care being the most thorough possible regardless of cost. Both know that most of the bill can be passed on to the third party. Questions about whether to do additional tests or procedures of marginal benefit tend to be resolved affirmatively if the cost to the patient is not an issue. Moreover, even a patient who is paying part of the bill does not normally know what care is necessary or appropriate.

The growth of health insurance, including generous plans with little or no patient cost sharing, has been encouraged by the tax system. Health insurance and other fringe benefits are treated as costs by companies and are not part of the worker's taxable income. Hence, especially in high-wage industries, workers have an incentive to take pay increases in the form of untaxed health insurance, rather than in the form of wages on which taxes must be paid.

Federal and state tax subsidies to the health care system (mostly from not taxing employer-provided health insurance) are estimated to be about $75 billion in 1992. Upper-income households get much bigger subsidies than lower-income ones, both because their tax rates are higher and because they are more likely to have employer-provided insurance.[4]

The cost problem is compounded by rapid advances in medical knowledge, which have led to the development of elaborate equipment and increasingly sophisticated and costly medical procedures. Hospitals and other providers often compete to have the latest technology, even if they cannot utilize it efficiently. The tendency of health providers to practice defensive medicine— ordering excessive tests out of fear of lawsuits—also adds to the costs passed on to third parties.

Medical care has been absorbing an increasing portion of the nation's resources for several decades. Many ideas for slowing the growth of costs have been suggested and some have been tried. Unfortunately, the main conclusion from these efforts is that piecemeal approaches do not work.

Increasing supply. If the price of some good or service is rising rapidly, common sense would dictate increasing the supply so the price will go down. One might think that increasing the supply of doctors would cause them to compete more vigorously with each other and result in lower fees. In fact, however, having more doctors appears to result in more medical

4. The federal tax for employer-provided health insurance was worth about $1,560 to the average household in the top quintile of household income in 1992 and about $525 to the average household in the second quintile. C. Eugene Steuerle, "Finance-Based Reform: The Search for Adaptable Health Policy," paper prepared for American Enterprise Institute conference on American Health Policy: Critical Issues for Reform (Washington: Urban Institute, October 1991), fig. 4.

services being delivered, not in lower prices. The number of physicians per 1,000 people in the United States rose from 1.6 in 1970 to 2.4 in 1990.[5] More people saw doctors more often, but physicians' incomes continued to rise.

Similarly, when the supply of hospital and nursing home beds increases, more people tend to be admitted to hospitals and nursing homes. Many parts of the country now have excess hospital beds. The unfilled beds, however, lead to higher, not lower hospital charges, since the large fixed costs of hospitals have to be spread over fewer patients.

Cost sharing. One might think that requiring patients to pay more of the cost of medical care out of their own pockets (through coinsurance and deductibles) would make both patients and providers more cost conscious and reduce excessive use of care. Indeed, higher out-of-pocket costs do reduce the use of care, but may cause some people to forgo medical attention they really need or impose severe hardships on those with limited resources and serious health problems. Moreover, many people dislike exposure to the risk of incurring unpredictable out-of-pocket costs. Faced with substantial coinsurance and deductibles, those who can afford it buy additional insurance to plug the gaps. Most middle- and upper-income older people have "medigap" insurance to cover coinsurance, deductibles, and other expenses not paid by medicare.

Changing incentives. Another approach has been to change the way providers are reimbursed. Fee-for-service billing gives doctors and other health providers an incentive to deliver more services—office visits, tests, procedures—in order to make more money. Health maintenance organizations (HMOs), by contrast, are groups of physicians and other health workers, often affiliated with a hospital, that agree to provide members with comprehensive health services for a fixed annual fee. An HMO has no reason to encourage nonessential services. In fact, it has an incentive to emphasize prevention and early detection of problems since the HMO loses money if its members' health deteriorates to the point of needing hospitalization or other

5. Congressional Budget Office, *Rising Health Care Costs: Causes, Implications, and Strategies* (April 1991), p. xii.

expensive forms of care. There is evidence that HMOs hold down hospitalization rates, although the evidence that they reduce overall health costs is weaker. In any case, such organizations are not available everywhere and are not to everyone's liking. Many patients prefer the freedom to choose their own doctor or other health provider.

Controlling parts of the system. Finally, one would think that the third parties themselves (since they pay the bills) would be able to hold down costs by controlling the use of care or the reimbursement rates of hospitals, doctors, and other health providers. Indeed, public-sector third parties have made major efforts to control the costs of their piece of the system, and private-sector ones are beginning to do so as well.

In 1983 Congress legislated a drastic change in the way medicare reimburses hospitals. Under its prospective payment system, medicare pays the hospital not for the actual cost of treating a particular patient, but an amount specified in advance for treating a patient with a particular diagnosis or set of diagnoses. This system (also known as the DRG system for "diagnosis related groups") gives the hospital an incentive to restore patients to health as rapidly as possible, even, it is alleged, to send them home too soon. The DRG system successfully reduced the rate of growth of medicare hospital expenditures, although there is evidence that hospitals have shifted costs from medicare to other payers and that some procedures formerly done in hospitals are now performed on an outpatient basis. In January 1992, medicare introduced a new payment schedule for physicians that may reduce the rate of increase in doctors' bills.

Medicaid programs have also set fee schedules and reimbursement rates that have held down cost growth. Medicaid rates are so low, however, that many doctors refuse to accept medicaid patients, who tend to have hard-to-treat health problems associated with poverty. Many hospitals and nursing homes are also reluctant to admit patients dependent on medicaid.

For a long time, private insurers did little to control costs, preferring simply to pass on the bills in the form of higher premiums. Recently, however, resistance by employers to escalating insurance premiums has forced both insurance companies and employers into strenuous efforts to control the use of medical care and the cost of providing it. Managed care systems require prior approval by the third party before a patient can be hospitalized, undergo surgery, or obtain other costly services. The administrative costs of these controls are extremely high for both insurers and providers. Most have not been operating long enough for definitive evaluation.

Comprehensive cost controls. Piecemeal control of medical care costs breaks down in a system with many payers. If medicare pays less than the full cost of treating medicare patients, providers pass the cost along to patients with private insurance. If providers find medicaid rates unattractive, they can refuse to treat medicaid patients. If private insurers attempt to manage care too strictly or hold down reimbursement rates, they lose customers or providers, or both. The American system of paying for health care seems designed not to promote efficiency and cost reduction, but to thwart efforts to achieve either.

The rapidly escalating cost of health care and the failure of fragmented efforts to control it have brought many people to the conclusion that cost control must be systemwide. The government must set reimbursement rates for health providers that apply to all payers, and increases in reimbursement rates must be controlled to hold down the rate of increase in total expenditures for health care.

Public regulation of the health care prices paid by all payers does not require that the government provide the services, or even that there be a national system of health insurance. It simply means that the government sets the rates that doctors, hospitals, and other providers can charge and that all providers have to accept these rates, whether they are paid by the government, a private insurer, or the patient. "Balance billing" (charging the patient for costs not reimbursed by the third party) is ruled out.

Several industrial countries have successfully controlled the increase in health care costs by national regulation. Their health care spending is also rising, but not nearly as rapidly as in the United States. In Germany, France, and Japan, most physicians are in private practice and are compensated on a fee-for-service basis.[6] There are both public and private hospi-

6. GAO, *Health Care Spending Control.*

tals. Most people obtain health insurance for themselves and their dependents through their employer. Patients can choose their own doctors or hospitals. In Germany and Japan, there are many insurers or payers; in France there are fewer.

In all three countries, health insurance coverage is universal and health technology is sophisticated. Upward pressure on spending would be enormous if there were no effective controls. In each country, however, fee schedules or reimbursement rates are set to constrain overall health spending to a target level. There is a formal process for setting the rates; representatives of the providers play a part; and all payers abide by the same payment rules.

All-payer reimbursement rates could be adopted in the United States in a variety of ways. Since medicare has the most comprehensive cost control system in current use, medicare's reimbursement system for physicians, hospitals, and other providers could be adapted for use by all payers, both public and private.[7] The National Leadership Coalition for Health Care Reform proposes a system that would start with a national health review board setting a target for total health expenditures. Expenditures would be targeted to grow more slowly each year until they were growing no faster than the economy. The board would set payment rates for all health services "after hearings and in consultation with affected parties" at levels estimated to keep overall health care spending below the expenditure target.[8] States could set up their own systems as long as their spending did not rise faster than the national target rate.

Henry Aaron has proposed a "single-payer" system, under which states or groups of states would designate "financial agents" for health care.[9] The federal government would set spending targets nationally and for each state or region. The

7. For estimates of the effect on total costs, see Terri Menke, *Universal Health Insurance Coverage Using Medicare's Payment Rates* (Washington: Congressional Budget Office, December 1991).

8. The National Leadership Coalition for Health Care Reform, "Excellent Health Care for All Americans at a Reasonable Cost: A Proposal for Three-Dimensional Health Care Reform" (Washington, 1991), p. 23.

9. Henry J. Aaron, *Serious and Unstable Condition: Financing America's Health Care* (Brookings, 1991), pp. 142–43.

financial agents would set rates after negotiations with providers in their area and actually pay all bills on behalf of insurers. Under this single-payer system, providers would not only receive the same rates, they would be paid from the same source. Hospitals, doctors, and other providers would be spared the costs and complexities of dealing with multiple payers.

The potential savings from controlling health costs in the United States are enormous. For example, if the United States had spent the same share of its gross domestic product on health care in 1991 as Canada was expected to spend (8.7 percent), it would have had $241 billion for other uses.[10] If it held spending at that proportion of GDP, instead of letting it rise to the 17.5 percent that some expect by 2000, cumulative savings over the decade would total more than $4 trillion (in 1991 prices).

These numbers are unrealistic because such drastic changes in such a short time are infeasible. However, they dramatize an important point: the health sector is so large and growing so rapidly that slowing its growth without jeopardizing health has huge potential for improving the American standard of living. Indeed, cutting the rate of growth of health care costs in half would enable the country to devote about 2 percent of GNP to other purposes by the end of the decade. The potential health cost dividend is larger than the potential peace dividend. The defense budget was less than half the size of the health sector in 1991 and already declining.

Even moderate slowing of the growth in health costs would ease some of the distress with America's health payment system. Employers' health costs would not rise so rapidly. Smaller firms would be less likely to drop health insurance (especially if insurance reforms made it easier for small firms to join larger risk pools with lower rates). The ranks of the uninsured might stop growing. Medicaid costs would not be such a rapidly escalating burden on taxpayers. Many millions of people, however, would still be left without adequate health insurance protection.

10. Jack A. Meyer, Sharon Silow-Carroll, and Sean Sullivan, *A National Health Plan in the U.S.: The Long-Term Impact on Business and the Economy* (Washington: Economic and Social Research Institute, 1991), pp. 18–19.

Moving to Universal Coverage

The case for universal access to health care rests on humanitarian and fairness arguments as well as on the economy's need for a healthy labor force. In a modern economy, everyone ought to have health insurance that covers preventive medicine, necessary treatment for acute illness by hospitals, physicians, and other providers, and long-term care for chronic illness and disability. The United States could move from its present system to universal coverage in a variety of ways. Two major strategies have strong advocates: national health insurance and "play or pay." Both options would require comprehensive cost controls.

National health insurance. The federal government would provide everyone with standard health insurance benefits, paid out of tax revenues, that would substitute for most employer-based insurance as well as for medicaid. National health insurance represents a drastic change from the current system. It would break the link between health insurance and employment. A worker who was laid off would still have health insurance. No one would have to worry that taking a different job or moving to a new part of the country would jeopardize the family's health insurance protection. National health insurance would also break the link between welfare and health benefits. No one would have to stay on welfare for fear of losing medicaid.[11] No one would be denied care because they had an undesirable form of coverage, such as medicaid, or no coverage at all.

Since national health insurance would pay all providers in the same way from the same source, paperwork would be greatly reduced for patients, providers, and employers. Patients would simply present their insurance card. Providers would be reimbursed by the government, and they could not bill patients for additional amounts. Employers would no longer need to devote vast amounts of time and expertise to the problems of employee health benefits. Doctors, hospitals, and other providers would

---

11. If there were significant cost sharing (for example, 20 percent coinsurance up to an annual limit), provision would have to be made for assisting low-income people with these payments.

no longer have to deal with a large number of payers; instead they would send their bills to the same place for payment. Their administrative costs would be substantially reduced.

The other side of the coin is that these changes would cause massive disruption of current arrangements and the loss of many jobs. Private insurance companies would have to get out of the health insurance business.[12] These companies would lay off or reassign employees who market, manage, and process health insurance. The government would be hiring workers to run the national health plan and might contract with insurance companies to process the claims, but the marketing and advertising functions of the current system would disappear.

Play or pay. The government would offer employers a choice between providing the same standard (or better) health insurance themselves or contributing to a fund that would provide the standard health insurance benefits for anyone who did not have insurance, including those currently on medicaid. Since it would retain the traditional link between employment and health insurance, "play or pay" would involve far less disruption of current patterns. Private insurers would still market health insurance to companies that elected to "play." Employees of those companies would retain a choice of plans, with all the advantages and complexities (for themselves, employers, and providers) that such choice entails.

A crucial decision would be how much employers who chose not to offer health insurance would have to pay into the backup fund for the uninsured. If the tax were set below the estimated cost of providing the insurance (including the administrative costs of managing their own health benefits), many firms might elect to pay rather than play. The National Leadership Coalition for Health Care Reform, which advocates such a plan, suggests a 9 percent payroll tax for nonplayers (employers would pay 7.25 percent and employees 1.75 percent). They estimate that at this rate high-wage employers would still offer their own health insurance benefits, but low-wage employers would find it advantageous to opt out, pay the tax, and have their employees

12. A small market for health insurance would still exist if the national health insurance excluded some kinds of health care.

covered by the public plan. It is hard to estimate how many firms and employees would end up in each category.

Comparing the approaches. Because "pay or play" would retain employer-based plans, it would involve smaller costs for the government than national health insurance. The total cost of a "play or pay" system to the economy as a whole, however, would probably be higher since private insurers would still be incurring the marketing cost of selling their competing plans. Companies electing to "play" would still have the administrative costs of health insurance, although these would be simplified by cost controls that applied to all payers.

The impact on the economy's total health care bill of moving to universal coverage, through either national health insurance or "play or pay," will depend largely on the effectiveness of comprehensive cost control. With effective regulation of cost growth, universal coverage could be achieved within a total health budget that was a significantly lower percentage of national output than currently projected. Without effective cost control, moving to universal coverage will only exacerbate the growth of total spending.

The two systems, however, would distribute the costs differently. "Play or pay" perpetuates the regressivity of reliance on private health insurance—at least for those who choose to "play." Under "play or pay," as under private health insurance, each employer pays a lump sum to purchase a standard health benefit package for each employee. In a competitive economy, such costs tend to reduce cash wages below what they would have otherwise been. A lump-sum payment reduces low wages disproportionately because the sum is a higher percentage of low wages than of high wages. A proportional payroll tax (even if paid by employers) tends to reduce cash wages proportionately. Hence the regressivity of "play or pay" would be mitigated to the extent that employers opted to pay a proportional payroll tax rather than the lump-sum payment.

The cost of national health insurance could be distributed in various ways depending on the taxes chosen to finance the program. Payroll tax financing is attractive because it distributes the burden proportionately to wages and emphasizes the contribution that employees are making to their own health insurance.

However, some would argue that adding an additional payroll tax to the existing taxes for social security and medicare would penalize employment. They would argue for financing a national plan at least partially out of general revenue, perhaps adding a value-added tax for the purpose.[13]

Whichever approach is taken, a major issue will be how to cover nursing home care and other long-term care for those with chronic disabilities. At present, long-term care bills are paid primarily by medicaid and patients themselves, with minor amounts coming from private insurers and medicare. If a variant of "play or pay" were adopted, medicare would probably be retained as a separate social insurance program for the elderly or disabled, subject to the same controls as the rest of the health system. Medicare could be broadened to include additional long-term care benefits. If the national health insurance route were taken, long-term care benefits could be provided as part of the basic benefit package. National health insurance should probably fold in medicare to avoid the costs of maintaining two social insurance systems.

As this discussion illustrates, finding a solution to America's health payment crisis is not going to be easy. The fragmented system now in place is so complex that transforming it into something more workable is an inherently complicated problem with many uncertainties and conflicting interests to be resolved. Despite the difficulties, however, devising a new system that will both slow the growth of costs and provide universal coverage is crucial to the future of the economy. It is a challenge that can best be met at the national level. It should be high on the federal government's priority list.

STRENGTHENING SOCIAL SECURITY

Social security is one of America's biggest successes. It has dramatically improved the quality of life for older Americans.

13. Henry Aaron, whose health insurance proposal is closer to "play or pay," advocates a federal value-added tax, which would pay part of the costs of health insurance and also make a contribution to the reduction of the federal deficit. Aaron, *Serious and Unstable Condition*, p. 147.

Fifty years ago, few elderly people could afford to retire and those who were not working were dependent on their own savings or relatives or charity. A large proportion were destitute. Now most older people have retirement incomes that allow them to live decently and independently. The poverty rate for Americans over 65 has dropped precipitously, and much of the credit goes to social security (see figure 4-4).

Despite the success and popularity of social security, proposals for amending it abound. Some would make fundamental changes, such as restricting the benefits to those who can show need. Others would reduce benefits by cutting the cost of living adjustments, raising the retirement age, or taxing benefits more fully. Others would reduce the system's reserves by cutting the payroll tax or would use the reserves to fix the roads or invest in private industry.

This section attempts to sort out the confusing array of conflicting proposals. My basic contention is that social security needs only marginal adjustment, not fundamental reform. Benefits should be taxed like private pension benefits, but they should not be means-tested. Reserves should be protected and used to reduce the federal debt held by the public. The growth in future benefit levels should be slowed by reducing the growth in initial benefits or raising the retirement age, not by cutting cost of living adjustments for people already retired.

How Social Security Works

In concept, social security is elegantly simple: working people pay a percentage of their wages (matched by their employers) into a trust fund and are entitled to benefits when they retire or become disabled. Survivors get help if a breadwinner dies. The tax rates and benefit levels are adjusted so that the system pays for itself—the tax collections plus interest earned on reserves are sufficient to pay for benefits and administrative expenses.[14]

Because they contributed, beneficiaries see social security

14. Administrative expenses were less than 1 percent of total benefit payments in 1990. *1991 Annual Report of the Federal Old-Age and Survivors Insurance and Disability Insurance Trust Fund*, H. Doc. 102-88, 102 Cong. 1 sess. (Government Printing Office, 1991), p. 26.

checks as something they have earned, not as subsidies or welfare. The relationship between benefits and contributions, however, is not simple. Benefits are related to prior earnings, but the formula by which the benefits are calculated is more generous to those with low earnings than to those with high ones. A retired aeronautical engineer gets a bigger social security check than a retired dishwasher because the engineers's earnings were higher. However, the difference in their social security checks is less than proportional to the difference in their past earnings. The system is designed to reduce the inequalities of life somewhat, without the indignity of charity.

The relatively generous treatment of people with modest wages has not occasioned much comment or protest, in part because almost all those now drawing social security benefits— rich and poor alike—are getting back far more than they contributed during their working lives. When the system was starting up, lots of workers were paying into the fund and few had retired. Surpluses tended to build up even at fairly low tax rates. Congress saw an inexpensive opportunity to raise the benefits of those who had already retired and did so frequently during the 1950s and 1960s. After a particularly large election-year increase in social security benefits in 1972, Congress, realizing that continuing the benefit hikes would eventually make the system too expensive, restricted future benefit increases to the inflation rate. Since then, social security recipients have received an annual cost of living adjustment (COLA), based on changes in the consumer price index, but no increases in real benefits. Social security tax rates have risen substantially in recent years, but most current retirees paid into the system when tax rates were lower. They are therefore getting considerable windfalls. These windfalls will gradually disappear as those who made bigger contributions join the ranks of retirees.

The Appropriate Level of Reserves

A social insurance system is different from a private company's pension plan. The company might go bankrupt and be unable to pay the claims of its retirees. Hence its pension fund needs enough reserves to pay the accumulated claims of beneficiaries even if no additional contributions are made by the company. The U.S. government, by contrast, will not go out of business. Payroll tax revenues will continue to flow into the social security trust funds, and tax rates can always be raised to higher levels if necessary. Social security can operate on a pay-as-you-go basis, using current revenues to pay current benefit claims. It need only keep sufficient reserves to ensure timely payments if a recession or some other event reduces payroll tax collections unexpectedly.

For much of its early history, social security operated on a pay-as-you-go basis with a comfortable reserve for contingencies. By the early 1980s, however, social security reserves were running low even by pay-as-you-go standards. Slower economic growth had lowered tax collections below earlier expectations, and inflation had raised benefit payments. Something had to be done to keep social security from running out of money. After a great deal of procrastination and political posturing, action was taken in 1983 not only to solve the immediate problem, but also to accumulate substantial reserves in anticipation of the retirement of the baby boom generation. These reserves will allow social security to fund some of the expected rise in benefit claims and avoid steep increases in payroll taxes when the baby boomers begin retiring around 2010.

In the 1990s and in the first two decades of the next century, social security is expected to run substantial annual surpluses and accumulate massive reserves. Eventually, however, these reserves will begin to drop as retirement claims exceed revenues. Unless tax rates are increased or benefits are reduced, the fund is expected to exhaust its reserves in about 2041.[15]

All long-run projections, of course, are subject to great uncertainty. If productivity grows more slowly than now expected, payroll tax collections will be lower than now anticipated. If longevity increases faster than projected, benefits will be higher than now estimated. Either of these shifts (or both together) could cause reserves to be exhausted before 2041. Nevertheless, the projections make two points clear. Social security is not in imminent danger of running out of money: there is ample time

15. *1991 Annual Report of the Federal OASDI Trust Fund*, H. Doc. 102-88, p. 94.

to consider when and how to add to the reserves. And, eventually, payroll tax increases will be needed if the current structure of benefits is to be maintained. There is no getting around the fact that a generous pension system in an aging society is expensive.

Social Security and National Saving

As discussed in chapter 5, the low level of national saving in the United States is a serious worry. National saving plummeted in the 1980s as private saving fell and the federal budget deficit (negative saving by the government) escalated (table 4-1). If low saving rates continue, the American standard of living is likely to grow slowly. Productive investment is likely to be low, and American capital will increasingly be owned by foreigners.

The bright spot in the otherwise bleak outlook for American saving is that social security will add substantially to national saving over the next several decades. Channeling these savings into productive investment would enhance future growth in incomes. At present, however, the social security surpluses are being used to finance the ongoing expenses of the government. These may be worthy expenditures, but in general they are not investments that raise future income.

If the rest of the government budget were at or near balance, the social security reserves could be used to buy back existing government debt from the public. More funds would be available for private investment. Interest rates would tend to fall. More investment projects would be undertaken. Productive use of the social security reserves thus depends on moving toward balance in the rest of the government budget by raising general taxes, cutting other expenditures, or some of each. Devolution of some federal responsibilities to the states would contribute to this goal.

Some have suggested that instead of buying government bonds, the social security system should finance productive investment directly by buying private securities. Such a policy shift, however, would do nothing to increase funds available for private investment. If the Treasury were unable to sell bonds to the social security system, it would have to borrow more from the public. Moreover, it is not in the American tradition to make a government agency a big shareholder in private companies or an owner of private, state, or local securities. Such ownership would concentrate too much economic power in Washington. A better way for the government to add to funds available for private investment is to run a budget surplus and reduce federal debt held by the public.

Senator Daniel P. Moynihan feels so strongly that the Treasury should not borrow social security reserves that he has advocated cutting the payroll tax and returning to pay-as-you-go financing in social security.[16] Moynihan and his supporters argue that social security payroll taxes should be used for social security. Building reserves would make sense if the reserves were used to reduce federal debt, but using them to finance general government expenses is unfair and misleading. Moreover, the payroll tax falls more heavily on low-income workers than does the income tax. It may be justifiable to use the payroll tax to fund social security, which returns relatively generous benefits to low-wage workers, but is not justifiable to use it to finance general government expenditures.

Senator Moynihan has identified a real problem but proposed the wrong remedy. Cutting the payroll tax would increase total government borrowing. Interest rates would rise; private, state, and local investment would become more expensive. What should be cut is not the payroll tax, but the general fund deficit.

Should the Growth in Benefits Be Reduced?

One frequently hears that reducing the budget deficit requires cutting middle-class entitlements, of which the largest is social security. Since social security is running annual surpluses, however, it is mitigating, not aggravating, the overall budget deficit. It is hard to make a convincing case for cutting social security benefits in the name of deficit reduction, since this move would involve using the payroll tax to finance an even larger portion of general government expenditures. If the payroll tax were cut commensurately, the budget deficit would be unaffected unless lowering the social security tax made people more willing to pay other kinds of taxes.

16. *Social Security Tax Cut*, Hearings before the Senate Committee on Finance, 101 Cong. 2 sess. (GPO, 1990).

A more cogent argument for slowing the growth in benefits, however, relates to decisions about national priorities. Thanks in part to social security, the economic status of older people has greatly improved in recent years while younger people have fallen behind. The proportion of children who are poor is rising while the incidence of poverty among the elderly is declining (figure 4-4). As the number of older people rises, the share of the federal budget—or of total national output—they command will grow, and the resources devoted to the well-being of younger people are likely to decline further.

The large portion of the population scheduled to draw social security benefits in, say, 2020, will absorb a substantial part of the resources produced by the economy in that year, whether or not the social security system has been adequately funded in advance. If the system were running on a pay-as-you-go basis, payroll taxes on the earnings of people working in 2020 would obviously have to be high enough to cover the benefits paid to retirees. Since the system will have built up reserves by running surpluses while the baby boomers are still working, these reserves can be used to pay the benefits. The reserves, however, are invested in government bonds. Hence general tax rates will have to be raised to allow the Treasury to pay off the bonds held by the social security system. The resources to pay the social security benefits have to come from somewhere—either from payroll taxes or from the general taxpayer.

The magnitude of the future claims of retirees argues for giving high priority to increasing productivity so a larger national income will be available out of which to pay these claims. Since no one can be sure these efforts will be successful, however, it seems prudent to reduce future commitments to the elderly or at least to reduce the rate of increase. It will always be possible to raise benefits if rapid productivity increases make extra resources available.

There are at least three approaches to reducing the increase in future social security benefits: cut the adjustment of benefits for inflation, reduce increases in initial benefits of retirees, or subject a larger portion of the benefits to income taxation. Of these, cutting inflation indexing is the most discussed and the least fair.

Cutting COLAs. Social security checks are increased each year to compensate for inflation, as measured by the consumer price index (CPI). Many proposals for reducing future social security benefits involve reducing the COLA to, say, the CPI minus 2 percent. In other words, social security beneficiaries would be asked to absorb the first 2 percent of inflation. Cutting COLAs is an unfair way of reducing benefits because it discriminates against the very old. Unless inflation were less than 2 percent, social security beneficiaries would have the real value of their benefits eroded by 2 percent each year. People in their nineties who had been retired for thirty years would have pitifully inadequate benefits, while recent retirees would suffer less.

Reducing initial benefits. A much fairer approach is to change the formula by which benefits are calculated so that initial benefits are slightly smaller in relation to prior earnings. Subsequent benefits would continue to be adjusted for changes in the cost of living.

A related approach, which could be combined with the last, is to provide an incentive for people to keep working by raising the age at which a retiree is eligible for full benefits and reducing benefits for those who retire early. Congress has already enacted an increase in the retirement age from 65 to 67 in gradual steps beginning in 2000. This change could be accelerated and the retirement age raised further, perhaps to 70 sometime in the next century.

Taxing more of social security benefits. A frequent criticism of social security is that high-income people receive benefits they do not need and that half these benefits are tax free. Some would like to cut out benefits to upper-income people altogether by means-testing the benefits to make sure they go only to those in need. Means-testing, however, would turn social security into a welfare program, which is both undesirable and politically infeasible. Support for social security is strong precisely because it is not a welfare program.

There is no reason, however, why social security benefits should not be taxed like private pensions. Indeed, Congress took the first step in that direction in the 1983 social security reforms. Until then social security benefits had been entirely tax free.

Beginning in 1984, half the benefits became taxable for single taxpayers with incomes over $25,000 and couples with incomes over $32,000.[17] The proceeds of the tax on benefits go into the social security fund.

The government would recoup more revenue if the tax rules that apply to private pensions were also applied to social security—once people got back what they put into the system, additional benefits would be fully taxable. This change would recoup part of the unneeded benefits of high-income people without much effect on low-income beneficiaries.

In sum, maintaining a strong social security system should be a high priority for the federal government. The system does not need fundamental change. Benefits should be taxable and their future growth slowed. The projected buildup in reserves should be protected, not undermined by a payroll tax cut. The social security surpluses, combined with defense expenditure cuts, health cost controls, and devolution of programs to the states, could then move the total federal budget into surplus, add to national saving, and encourage productive investment.

17. *Overview of Entitlement Programs*, Committee Print, p. 26. About 22 percent of social security recipients were affected in 1922.

TEN

Federalism Faces New Challenges

The greatest impediment to reviving the American dream is that Americans have lost confidence in their ability to control their own destiny. A nation long noted for its "can-do" spirit—for self-assurance often bordering on cockiness—has become mired in pessimism and self-deprecation.

It has become fashionable, indeed almost obligatory, to predict decline in America's economic strength and stagnation in its standard of living. Those who view with alarm often voice inconsistent fears. They worry that America's manufacturing jobs will be lost to low-productivity countries like Mexico or India, where unskilled peasants are willing to do repetitive jobs for little money. At the same time, they predict that the United States will be unable to keep up with high-productivity, high-wage countries like Japan and the members of the European Economic Community, whose workers are more skilled, factories more automated, and transportation systems more efficient than America's.

Frustration and foreboding about the economy have erupted in popular anger at the political system, especially at the federal level, but few believe that public officials will take steps to reverse the gloomy economic outlook. Again, attitudes are inconsistent. People blame Washington both for excessive interference with private initiatives and for failure to provide economic direction and leadership. They criticize Congress and federal executives for being out of touch with real people and not caring what ordinary citizens think. At the same time, they castigate officials for being too political and doing only what is popular with voters. Pundits bemoan lack of leadership, while predicting that Americans would reject any potential leader who asked them to make sacrifices or work hard to improve future performance.

To visitors from less favored parts of the world, all this defeatism and self-criticism must seem both mystifying and counterproductive. There are no objective reasons for such discouragement about America's economic future, unless the low expectations themselves become self-fulfilling. The United States has enormous natural and human resources and a stunning record of performance and creativity. Americans still have the world's highest productivity and standard of living. The challenges facing the American economic system today are not especially daunting compared with challenges that it has met in the past or that face many other economies today.

Americans responded vigorously to economic collapse during the Great Depression and strengthened their economic institutions in the process. They geared up rapidly for unprecedented levels of production in World War II and sustained the long, costly effort to contain communism for more than four decades. The American economy over the years has proved extraordinarily resilient in absorbing and training millions of new workers over fairly short periods—including waves of immigration, migrants from farm to city, the large baby boom generation, and an influx of women. Industry and communities have adapted to life-changing new technologies, including the railroad, the automobile, factory mass production, computers, and modern telecommunications.

The new challenges of modernizing education and infrastructure and revitalizing institutions, including government, will take effort, energy, and commitment, but so did the old ones. The chief obstacle to meeting the new challenges is not their inherent difficulty, but the widespread belief that Americans and their institutions are no longer capable of change and renewal. For the first time in their national history, Americans see themselves as helpless victims of circumstance, unable to take charge of their future.

THE ECONOMIC CHALLENGE

Reviving the American dream requires sustainable and widely shared increases in the standard of living. Private investment, embodying new technologies and processes, must move to a higher level. An increase in domestic saving is required to finance this investment without continuing to depend on foreign capital. To generate the higher level of domestic saving, the federal budget should move from deficit to surplus. Moreover, increased public investment is needed to improve education and work skills, modernize infrastructure, and keep the country on the frontiers of science and technological change.

The federal government cannot simultaneously play a major role in new public investment and eliminate the deficit without a substantial federal tax increase. Such an increase seems unlikely to gain political support without a major shift in public attitudes. Moreover, the federal government is not well suited to take responsibility for improving education, training, and infrastructure or fostering economic development. These are functions of government that require experimentation, adaptation to local conditions, accountability of on-the-scene officials, and community participation and support. State and local governments are more likely than the federal government to carry out these functions successfully.

Hence an appealing strategy for implementing needed new domestic policies is "dividing the job" (see chapter 7). The federal government should do what it has proved it can do well: strengthen the nation's social insurance system. It should take on the dual task of controlling the growth of health costs and ensuring that everyone has health insurance. The states should take charge of the productivity agenda, especially education, training, infrastructure, and economic development, while the federal government should devolve its programs in these areas to the states. Devolution will help move the federal budget toward surplus.

Some federal tax increases will be needed, earmarked for the new health insurance plan so that taxpayers know what they are paying for. State revenue increases will also be needed to support the productivity agenda. States should strengthen their revenue systems by sharing the proceeds of one or more common taxes.

THE INSTITUTIONAL CHALLENGE

Reviving the American dream will take far more than sorting out functions among levels of government or even a major shift in economic policy. It will take revitalization of institutions of all sorts. If Americans are to recover their self-confidence and belief that positive changes are possible, they must change the institutions of the workplace and of government.

A revolution is in progress in American business management. Frightened by gloomy forecasts and spurred by foreign competitiveness, many American companies are restructuring themselves from the bottom up. This revolution has put enormous emphasis on improving the quality of products and services, increasing responsiveness to customers and clients, and empowering workers at all levels to contribute to company success. Productivity depends on workers' feeling that they make a difference to a team effort and have some control over results.

Another theme of the business revolution is that successful companies have well-defined missions. They develop expertise in a set of closely related lines of business. They do what they do very well and resist excursions into unrelated businesses where they do not have proven competence. Some unwieldy conglomerates have dissolved into more manageable units; few new ones are forming.

The business revolution is spilling over into government. Many of the themes are the same. Reformers in government emphasize the "entrepreneurial spirit," innovation, responsiveness to the public (seen as customers and clients), and empowerment of workers in a decentralized organization.[1] They also emphasize the importance of government agencies having clear missions and being accountable for results.

Revitalizing institutions, in both the public and private sectors, requires more than buzzwords and a few examples of conspicuous success. It will take pervasive commitment to continuous improvement, the breakdown of old hierarchies, and their replacement with new patterns of citizen and worker involvement. One ingredient should be a major effort to sort out functions of government—both between the federal government and the states and within the states—to clarify missions and make sure everyone knows who is responsible for which activities.

IMPROVING THE POLICY PROCESS

Reviving the American dream also involves restoring the public's sense of control over government and involvement in the policy process. There is plenty of evidence that many citizens feel left out. They perceive that they are on the receiving end of arbitrary government actions, not part of a democratic decisionmaking process. A great gulf has developed between the general public and politicians, government executives, and public policy experts.

An adversarial struggle exists between experts and the public on who will govern America. On one side are the experts—smaller in number and weaker than the public in formal power but holding an indispensable piece of the solution. As a group, these experts respect the institution of democracy and would be chagrined if their good faith were challenged. At the same time, however, their view of the general public is that it is ill informed and ill equipped to deal with the problems to which they, the experts, have devoted their lives.[2]

1. David Osborne and Ted Gaebler, *Reinventing Government: How the Entrepreneurial Spirit Is Transforming the Public Sector* (Addison-Wesley, 1992).
2. Daniel Yankelovich, *Coming to Public Judgment: Making Democracy Work in a Complex World* (Syracuse University Press, 1991), p. 4.

Part of any serious effort to bridge the gap between the public and the experts must be simplification and demystification of the policy process. The procedures for putting together the federal budget, for example, have become incredibly complicated. Partly as a result of competition between the president and Congress for control of the budget, and partly as a result of efforts to reduce the deficit, the federal budget process now involves so many actors, forecasts, rules, stages, and layers of decisions that even the participants have a hard time understanding what is going on. The complexity has exacerbated hostility toward government, since people who are mystified naturally assume something illicit is going on at their expense. Simplification of the budget process will not solve the deficit problem, but it is an important prerequisite to public understanding of the problem and options for solving it.

Similarly, the overlapping roles of state and federal government add to the public's mystification about the process of government and their sense of powerlessness. Sorting out functions between the federal and state levels should help clarify what different levels of government do and restore some confidence that voters' choices can actually affect what happens.

In sum, reviving the American dream will require not only new economic policies, but restoring individuals' sense that they can make a difference in their own lives and in the functioning of public and private institutions. America is indeed fortunate that the structure of its economy and its government makes such empowerment possible. It is far easier for individuals to make a difference in a free enterprise market system than in a centrally controlled economy. Similarly, there is far more scope for citizen participation and competitive reform in a federal structure than in a centralized top-down government.

There were good historical reasons why power flowed toward Washington from the 1930s to the beginning of the 1980s. Similarly, there are now equally cogent reasons for reexamining the federal structure and dividing responsibilities more clearly between the states and the national government: revitalizing the economy and making government work better.

Recommended Readings

CHAPTER ONE

Dionne, E. J., Jr. *Why Americans Hate Politics*. Simon and Schuster, 1991.

Krugman, Paul. *The Age of Diminished Expectations: U.S. Economic Policy in the 1990s*. MIT Press, 1990.

Osborne, David, and Ted Gaebler. *Reinventing Government: How the Entrepreneurial Spirit Is Transforming the Public Sector*. Addison-Wesley, 1992.

Yankelovich, Daniel. *Coming to Public Judgment: Making Democracy Work in a Complex World*. Syracuse University Press, 1991.

CHAPTER TWO

Aaron, Henry J., ed. *Setting National Priorities: Policy for the Nineties*. Brookings, 1990.

Hormats, Robert D. "The Roots of American Power," *Foreign Affairs*, vol. 70 (Summer 1991).

Mann, Thomas E., ed. *A Question of Balance: The President, the Congress, and Foreign Policy*. Brookings, 1990.

Mathews, Jessica Tuchman. "Redefining Security," *Foreign Affairs*, vol. 68 (Spring 1989).

McGuire, Martin D. "The Revolution in International Security," *Challenge*, vol. 33 (March–April 1990).

Moran, Theodore H. "International Economics and National Security," *Foreign Affairs*, vol. 69 (Winter 1990–91).

Nolan, Janne E. *Trappings of Power: Ballistic Missiles in the Third World*. Brookings, 1991.

Nye, Joseph S., Jr. *Bound to Lead: The Changing Nature of American Power*. Basic Books, 1990.

Peterson, Peter G., and James K. Sebenius. "The Primacy of the Domestic Agenda," in Graham Allison and Gregory F. Treverton, eds., *Rethinking America's Security: Beyond Cold War to a New World Order*. Norton, 1992.

Rivlin, Alice M., David E. Jones, and Edward C. Meyer. *Beyond Alliances: Global Security through Focused Partnership*. John D. and Catherine T. MacArthur Foundation and Rockefeller Foundation, October 1990.

Twentieth Century Fund. *Partners in Prosperity: The Report of the Twentieth Century Fund Task Force on the International Coordination of National Economic Policies.* New York: Priority Press Publications, 1991.

CHAPTERS THREE, FOUR, AND FIVE

An America That Works: The Life-Cycle Approach to a Competitive Work Force. New York: Committee for Economic Development, 1990.

Baily, Martin Neil, and Alok K. Chakrabarti. *Innovation and the Productivity Crisis.* Brookings, 1988.

Bosworth, Barry, Gary Burtless, and John Sabelhaus. "The Decline in Saving: Evidence from Household Surveys," *Brookings Papers on Economic Activity, 1:1991.*

Burtless, Gary, ed. *A Future of Lousy Jobs? The Changing Structure of U.S. Wages.* Brookings, 1990.

Congressional Budget Office. *The Economic and Budget Outlook: Fiscal Years 1993–1997.* January 1992.

Denison, Edward F. *Trends in American Economic Growth, 1929–1982.* Brookings, 1985.

Dertouzos, Michael L., Richard K. Lester, and Robert M. Solow. *Made in America: Regaining the Productive Edge.* MIT Press, 1989.

General Accounting Office. *The Budget Deficit: Outlook, Implications, and Choices.* OCG-90-5. September 1990.

Harris, Ethan S., and Charles Steindel. "The Decline in U.S. Saving and Its Implications for Economic Growth," *Federal Reserve Bank of New York Quarterly Review,* vol. 16 (Winter 1991).

Jaynes, Gerald David, and Robin M. Williams, Jr., eds. *A Common Destiny: Blacks and American Society.* Washington: National Academy Press, 1989.

Johnson, Clifford M., and others. *Child Poverty in America.* Washington: Children's Defense Fund, 1991.

Johnston, William B., and Arnold H. Packer. *Workforce 2000: Work and Workers for the Twenty-First Century.* Indianapolis: Hudson Institute, June 1987.

Kasten, Richard. *The Changing Distribution of Federal Taxes: 1975–1990.* Congressional Budget Office, October 1987.

Levy, Frank. *Dollars and Dreams: The Changing American Income Distribution.* Norton, 1988.

Levy, Frank, and Richard J. Murnane. "U.S. Earnings Levels and Earnings Inequality: A Review of Recent Trends and Proposed Explanations," *Journal of Economic Literature* (forthcoming, September 1992).

Litan, Robert E., Robert Z. Lawrence, and Charles L. Schultze, eds. *American Living Standards: Threats and Challenges*. Brookings, 1988.

Mathews, Jessica Tuchman, ed. *Preserving the Global Environment: The Challenge of Shared Leadership*. Norton, 1991.

Michel, Richard C. *Economic Growth and Income Equality since the 1982 Recession*. Washington: Urban Institute, August 1990.

Mishel, Lawrence R., and David M. Frankel. *The State of Working America*. M.E. Sharpe, 1991.

New World Dialogue on Environment and Development in the Western Hemisphere. *Compact for a New World: An Open Letter to the Heads of State and Government and Legislators of the Americas*. Washington: World Resources Institute, October 1991.

President's Commission on Industrial Competition. *Global Competition: The New Reality: The Report of the President's Commission on Industrial Competitiveness*. vols. I, II. Washington: Government Printing Office, January 1985.

Repetto, Robert and others. *Wasting Assets: Natural Resources in the National Income Accounts*. Washington: World Resources Institute, June 1989.

Small, Kenneth A., Clifford Winston, and Carol A. Evans. *Road Work: A New Highway Pricing and Investment Policy*. Brookings, 1989.

World Commission on Environment and Development. *Our Common Future*. Oxford University Press, 1987.

CHAPTERS SIX, SEVEN, & EIGHT

Aaron, Henry J., ed. *The Value-Added Tax: Lessons from Europe*. Brookings, 1981.

Beam, David R. "On the Origins of the Mandate Issue," in Michael Fix and Daphne A. Kenyon, eds., *Coping with Mandates: What Are the Alternatives?* Washington: Urban Institute Press, 1990.

———. "Reinventing Federalism: State-Local Government Roles in the New Economic Order." Paper prepared for the 1988 annual meeting of the American Political Science Association.

Beam, David R., Timothy Conlan, and David B. Walker. "Federalism: The Challenge of Conflicting Theories and Contemporary

Practice," in Ada W. Finifter, ed., *Political Science: The State of the Discipline*. Washington: American Political Science Association, 1983.

Beer, Samuel H., and others. *Federalism: Making the System Work*. Washington: Center for National Policy, 1982.

Bowman, Ann O'M., and Richard C. Kearney. *The Resurgence of the States*. Prentice-Hall, 1986.

Chubb, John E. "Federalism and the Bias for Centralization," in John E. Chubb and Paul E. Peterson, eds., *The New Direction in American Politics*. Brookings, 1985.

Conlan, Timothy J. *New Federalism: Intergovernmental Reform from Nixon to Reagan*. Brookings, 1988.

Dengel, Annette. "The Tax System of the Federal Republic of Germany." Brookings Discussion Papers in Economics, April 1986.

Derthick, Martha. "American Federalism: Madison's Middle Ground in the 1980s," *Public Administration Review*, vol. 47 (January–February 1987).

Elazar, Daniel J. *The American Partnership: Intergovernmental Cooperation in the Nineteenth-Century United States*. University of Chicago Press, 1962.

Gramlich, Edward M. "Reforming U.S. Federal Fiscal Arrangements," in John M. Quigley and David L. Rubinfeld, eds., *American Domestic Priorities: An Economic Appraisal*. University of California Press, 1985.

John, DeWitt. *Shifting Responsibilities: Federalism in Economic Development*. Washington: National Governors' Association, 1987.

King, Anthony, ed. *The New American Political System*. Washington: American Enterprise Institute Press, 1990.

Ladd, Helen F., and Fred C. Doolittle. "Which Level of Government Should Assist the Poor?" *National Tax Journal*, vol. 35 (September 1982).

Miller, John A. "State Administration of a National Sales Tax: A New Opportunity for Cooperative Federalism," *Virginia Tax Review*, vol. 9 (Fall 1989).

Musgrave, Richard A. *The Theory of Public Finance: A Study in Public Economy*. McGraw-Hill, 1959.

Musgrave, Richard A., and Peggy B. Musgrave. *Public Finance in Theory and and Practice*, 5th ed. (McGraw-Hill, 1989).

Nathan, Richard P., Fred C. Doolittle and Associates. *The Consequences of Cuts: The Effects of the Reagan Domestic Program on State and Local Governments*. Princeton Urban and Regional Research Center, 1983.

————. *Reagan and the States*. Princeton University Press, 1987.

O'Toole, Laurence J., Jr., ed. *American Intergovernmental Relations: Foundations, Perspectives, and Issues*. Washington: Congressional Quarterly, 1985.

Peterson, Paul E., Barry G. Rabe, and Kenneth K. Wong. *When Federalism Works*. Brookings, 1986.

Peterson, Paul E., and Mark C. Rom. *Welfare Magnets: A New Case for a National Standard*. Brookings, 1990.

Shannon, John, and James Edwin Kee. "The Rise of Competitive Federalism," *Public Budgeting and Finance*, vol. 9 (Winter 1989).

Sundquist, James L., with David W. Davis. *Making Federalism Work: A Study of Program Coordination at the Community Level*. Brookings, 1969.

Tait, Alan A. *Value Added Tax: International Practice and Problems*. Washington: International Monetary Fund, 1988.

Terra, Ben. *Sales Taxation: The Case of Value Added Tax in the European Community*. Boston: Kluwer Law and Taxation Publishers, 1988.

Van Horn, Carl E., ed. *The State of the States*. Washington: Congressional Quarterly, 1989.

Walker, David B. *Toward a Functioning Federalism*. Little, Brown, 1981.

CHAPTER NINE

Aaron, Henry J. *Serious and Unstable Condition: Financing America's Health Care*. Brookings, 1991.

Congressional Budget Office. *Rising Health Care Costs: Causes, Implications, and Strategies*. April 1991.

General Accounting Office. *Canadian Health Insurance: Lessons for the United States*. HRD-91-90. June 1991.

————. *Health Care Spending Control: The Experience of France, Germany, and Japan*. HRD-92-9. November 1991.

————. *Social Security: The Trust Fund Reserve Accumulation, the Economy, and the Federal Budget*. HRD-89-44. January 1989.

Van de Water, Paul N., ed. *Social Insurance Issues for the Nineties: Proceedings of the Third Conference of the National Academy of Social Insurance*. Dubuque, Iowa: Kendall Hunt, 1992.

Index

Aaron, Henry J., 163, 168n
Acid rain, 12, 24–25
Aid to families with dependent children (AFDC), 48, 90
  budget impact of, 98
  in "dividing the job" scenario, 119
  poorer states favored in, 136
  in Reagan swap proposal, 124
Air pollution, 56, 64, 67
  and gas tax, 146–47
Allen, Robert S., 92
American dream, 1
  and "dividing the job," 119
  fading of, 1–2
  reviving of, 179–82
Articles of Confederation, 83
Askew, Janice M., 69n

Baby boom generation, 45, 58, 72, 174
"Back to the sixties" scenario, 115–16
Baily, Martin Neil, 45n
Baker v. Carr, 105
Balance billing (health care), 162
Bank of Credit and Commerce International (BCCI), 24
Barro, Robert J., 135n
Beam, David R., 108, 120–21
Benker, Karen M., 130n
Beyle, Thad L., 92n, 94n, 103n, 104n
Blacks
  and civil rights revolution, 49, 94–95
  during "disappointing years," 60–61
  in "good news" period, 49
  and war on poverty, 95
Bowman, Ann O'M., 92n, 104n
Bracket creep, 107
Brown v. Board of Education, 95
Budget deficit. See Federal budget deficit
Building boom ("good news" years), 49–50
Bush, George, and international affairs, 30

Business management, revolution in, 180
Canada, health care system in, 157, 164
Carter, Jimmy, 101
Catalog sales, state attempts to tax, 139
Categorical grant programs, 92
  and New Federalism, 123
  proliferation of, 98–99, 100
  under Reagan, 101–02
  See also Grants, federal
Chakrabarti, Alok K., 45n
Children, poverty rate among, 48, 60
Civil rights movement, and federal growth, 86, 94–95
Cold war, 26–27
Committee for Economic Development, 103
Common shared state taxes, 8, 17–18, 118, 127, 142–52, 180
  corporate income, 18, 118–19, 145
  gasoline or energy, 18, 119, 145–47, 150
  implementation of, 147–50
  politics of, 151–52
  vs. revenue sharing, 125
  sales, 17–18, 127, 142–43
  value-added, 17–18, 118–19, 143–45
Communism, and cold war, 26–27
Community action programs, 96
Community development block grant program, 123
Compact, interstate, on common tax, 149, 152
Competitive federalism, 83–84
Comprehensive Employment and Training Act (1973), 123
Congress
  improved professional support for, 105
  and international issues, 30
Congressional Budget Office, 14, 105, 111

188

Constitution, U.S.
  drafting of, 83
  Fourteenth Amendment to, 105
  and income tax, 85
  school desegregation under, 95
  Tenth Amendment to, 83
Cooperative federalism, 83, 119
Corporate income tax, common
    shared state, 18, 118–19, 145

Democratic political system
  in American dream, 1
  paralysis of, 2, 7
  popular anger at, 15–16, 178
Dengel, Annette, 150n
Depreciation, and infrastructure,
    63–64
Devolution, 17, 102
  in "dividing the job" scenario, 118,
    125 (*see also* "Dividing the job"
    scenario)
  and federal budget, 17, 118, 180
  in Reagan swap proposal, 124
Dionne, E. J., Jr., 15n
"Disappointing years" (*1973*-present),
    57–58
  and blacks, 60–61
  and environment, 64
  and family structure, 61
  income distribution in, 59, 70–72
  and infrastructure, 63–64
  living standard in, 58–59
  and medical costs, 78–80
  poverty in, 42, 59–60
  and productivity, 59, 65–70
  and saving, investment, and inter-
    est rates, 61–63, 74–78
Discrimination, racial, by states, 93
Distribution of income
  and blacks, 49, 60–61, 95
  during "disappointing years," 59,
    60, 61
  and "dividing the job" scenario,
    122
  and economic expectations, 38–39
  during "good news" years, 45–46
  and rise of inequality (*1980*s), 70–
    72
  and tax subsidies on health insur-
    ance, 159
  See also Poverty

"Dividing the job" scenario, 116–22,
    125, 153, 179–80, 182
Divorce, 56, 90
Domestic policy, and global interde-
    pendence, 10–11, 30–31, 110
Doolittle, Fred, 101
DRG (diagnosis related group) sys-
    tem, 161
"Drift" scenario, 114–15
Dual federalism, 8, 83, 84–85
  "dividing the job" contrasted with,
    119
  and revenues, 136

Economic expectations
  cyclic vs. long-run, 32–33, 34–35
  and equality of income, 38–39
  and media, 33–34
  pessimistic, 4, 177–78
  and standard of living, 35–38 (*see
    also* Standard of living)
  and sustainability, 39–41
Economic history. *See* "Disappoint-
    ing years"; "Good News" years
Economic policy, growing consensus
    on, 6–8
Economic stabilization, from social
    insurance and welfare programs,
    90–91
Education
  bottom-up reform of, 11
  desegregation of, 95
  federal grants for, 92
  and inequality increase (*1970*s and
    *1980*s), 72
  and productivity decline (*1970*s),
    67–68
  and productivity improvement,
    68–69
  reform of, 72–74
"Eighties continued" scenario,
    111–15
Elazar, Daniel J., 85n
Elderly
  during "disappointing years,"
    59–60, 71
  poverty rate for, 48, 60, 169
  and public spending ("good news"
    years), 50–51
  and social security, 59, 168–69, 174

Elementary and Secondary Education Act, 96, 136
Entitlement programs
and budget deficit, 173
vs. discretionary spending, 102
in "good news" years, 50
social insurance and welfare as, 89
Environment
and "disappointing years," 64
and economic growth sustainability, 40–41
and "good news" years, 55–56
as national security dimension, 24–25
resources required for protecting, 38
Equality, economic. *See* Distribution of income
European Economic Community
competition from, 177
uniformity of taxes, 151
value-added tax in, 143
Evans, Carol A., 40n, 70n, 146n
Evolution of federalism. *See* Historical evolution of federalism
Executive branch of state government, reform of, 102–05

Family assistance plan, of Nixon, 98, 123
Family structure
during "disappointing" years, 61
during "good news" period, 56
and welfare programs, 90
Federal budget deficit, 13–14, 81
and common shared state tax, 152
in "dividing the job" scenario, 118
escalation of ("disappointing years"), 9, 61–62
during "good news" years, 52–53
projection of, 111
and saving, 7, 17, 75, 77, 179
and social security surpluses, 78, 172, 173
and state fiscal recoveries, 130
Federal government
appropriate roles for, 12, 153–54
inappropriate roles for, 12, 179
See also "Dividing the job" scenario

Federalism
"back to the sixties" scenario for, 115–16
and bottom-up vs. top-down reform, 11–13
changing views of, 8–10, 82–84 (*see also* Historical evolution of federalism)
and common shared state taxes, 17–18, 152 (*see also* Common shared state taxes)
and devolution, 17 (*see also* Devolution)
and dissatisfaction with government, 15–16, 109, 182
distinction of responsibilities needed in, 7–8, 19, 81, 110–11, 181
"dividing the job" scenario for, 116–22, 125, 153, 179–80, 182
"eighties continued" scenario for, 111–15
and international role, 11, 30–31
and mandates, 107–09, 113, 131
and mitigation of interstate inequalities, 135–36
and welfare programs, 90
Federalism, types of
competitive, 83–84
cooperative, 83, 119
dual, 8, 83, 84–85, 119, 136
Federal programs
for infrastructure, 50, 63, 99, 135–36 (*see also* Infrastructure)
in war on poverty, 95–98
social insurance, 88–89, 153, 154–56 (*see also* Social insurance)
welfare, 88, 89–90, 97, 98, 119
See also Grants, federal; *specific programs*
Federal Reserve System, 57, 58, 85
Federal spending. *See* Government spending, federal
Federal structure, global, 28
Finance, globalization of, 23–24
Fix, Michael, 108n
Florida, tax on services attempted in, 139–41

Food stamp program, 90, 98
under "dividing the job" scenario,
122
in Reagan swap proposal, 124
Ford, Gerald, 123
Foreign affairs. *See* Global interdependence; International trade,
U.S.
Foreign investment in the United
States, 6–7
dangers of, 74, 114–15
during *1986–90* period, 62–63
France, health care in, 157, 162–63

Gaebler, Ted, 18–19, 181n
Gasoline tax, common shared state,
145–47, 150
General revenue sharing (GRS) program, 100, 102, 125, 136. *See also*
Revenue sharing
Germany
health care in, 157, 162–63
shared taxes in, 18, 150–51
Global interdependence, 10–11, 20–21
and common shared taxes, 151,
152
and domestic policy, 11, 30–31,
110
implications of, 25–31
and national security, 21–25
and need for rising income, 37–38
and state industrial policy, 120–21
Global warming, 25
"Good news" years (*1940–73*), 42, 43
and blacks, 49
and environment, 55–56
and family structure, 56
government spending growth in,
50–53, 91
income distribution in, 45–46
living standard in, 43–45
poverty decline in, 46–49
private and public building boom
in, 49–50
and productivity, 45
saving, investment, and interest
rates in, 53–55
and taxes, 91
Government. *See* Federal government; State government; State
and local government

Government, dissatisfaction with,
15–16, 178, 181–82
Government programs. *See* Federal
programs; *specific programs*
Government regulation
for environment, 64
and productivity decline, 66–67
in Progressive era, 84–85
Government spending, federal
in "eighties continued" scenario,
113
in "good news" period, 50–53, 91
in *1960–90*, 75, 76
under Reagan, 101
See also Federal budget deficit
Government spending, state and local, 50–51, 85, 129–33
Gramlich, Edward M., 131n
Grants, federal
categorical, 92, 98–99, 100, 101–02,
123
economic development, 121–22
and mandates, 108
proliferation of, 87, 98–99, 100, 109
under Reagan, 101–02
redistributive, 121, 122, 135–36
for selected years (1960–90), 131
Great Depression, 46–47, 87, 120, 178
and growth of federal government,
8, 85, 86
and international trade, 88
and social insurance, 154
and state government, 92
and unemployment insurance, 89
and World War II, 43
Great Society programs, 92
Greenhouse gases, 25, 40
and gas tax, 147
Guaranteed income, 97–98
Gulf war, 10, 21, 23
debate over, 30
Gulick, Luther, 92

Head Start program, 11–12, 96, 136
Health care financing
cost control for, 13, 80, 81, 117,
157, 158–64
in "eighties continued" scenario,
114
as federal function, 8, 12–13, 17,
153–54

and federal spending rise, 113
rise in cost of, 7, 78–80, 157
Health insurance
    cost sharing (coinsurance and de-
        ductibles) in, 160
    inadequacy of coverage, 7, 79, 80,
        157
    increasing burden of, 157–58
    reform of, 156–68
    and tax system, 159
Health maintenance organizations
    (HMOs), 160–61
Heller, Walter, 99, 100n
Hirsch, Fred, 37n
Historical evolution of federalism, 8–
    10, 82–84
    dual federalism, 8, 84–85
    federal growth, 8–9, 85–87, 91–102
    institution building, 87–91
    reaction, 9–10, 101–02
    reform of state governments,
        102–07
Hoover, Herbert, 87

Income, family, during *1947–90* pe-
    riod, 44, 47, 58. *See also* Stand-
    ard of living
Income, per capita, 35–36
Income distribution. *See* Distribution
    of income
Industrial policy, 120–21
Inequality, economic. *See* Distribu-
    tion of income
Inflation, 39
    and bracket creep, 107
    during "disappointing" years, 57–
        58, 62
    during "good news" years, 55
Infrastructure
    and construction boom ("good
        news" years), 50
    deterioration of ("disappointing"
        years), 63–64
    and economic growth sustainabil-
        ity, 39–40, 81
    federal grants' effect on, 99
    and productivity improvement,
        69–70
    See also Transportation systems

Interest rates
    during "disappointing" years, 57–
        58, 62
    during "good news" years, 53–55
    real vs. nominal, 54–55
International finance, 23–24
International Monetary Fund, 26
International trade, U.S., 22–23
    and cold war, 26
    exports and imports (*1950–90*), 22
    and Great Depression, 88
Interstate compact, on common tax,
    149, 152
Investment
    during "disappointing years," 62
    by foreigners, 6–7, 62–63, 74, 114
    during "good news" years, 53–55
    for productivity growth, 6–7
    public, 63–64, 115
    and real interest rates, 55
Iraq, 27
Isolationism, as infeasible, 10

Japan
    as competitor, 27, 177
    health care in, 162–63
    as partner, 28
Jaynes, Gerald David, 49n
Jewell, Malcolm E., 94n, 106n
Johnson, Lyndon B., 92, 95, 97, 100

Kearney, Richard C., 92n, 104n
Kee, James Edwin, 84n, 107n
Keller, Morton, 92n
Kenyon, Daphne A., 108n
Koch, Edward I., 99, 108
Krugman, Paul, 4, 114–15

Land grants, 84
Lapointe, Archie E., 69n
Larson, Michael W., 130n
Lawrence, Robert Z., 44n
Legislative branch of state govern-
    ment, reform of, 105–07
Less developed countries, and envi-
    ronmental concerns, 40
Levy, Frank, 44n, 72n
Litan, Robert E., 44n
Living standard. *See* Standard of
    living

Local governments, and revenue sharing, 100. *See also* State and local
   government

Managed care systems (health care),
   162
Mandates by federal to state governments, 107–09, 113
   on medicaid, 109, 131
Manley, Richard A., 141
Manufacturing, productivity during
   "disappointing years," 59
Massachusetts, tax on services attempted in, 141–42
Mead, Nancy A., 69n
Means testing, 89
   vs. social insurance, 155
   for social security, 175
   and welfare, 89
Media economics, 33–34
Medicaid, 90, 98, 156–57
   cost control in, 161
   health insurance as supplanting,
      117
   link with welfare, 122, 165
   and "play or pay" system, 166
   poorer states favored in, 136
   projected increase for, 113
   in Reagan swap proposal, 124
   rising cost of, 158, 164
   and state fiscal burdens, 131, 133
Medical care. *See* Health care
Medicare, 50, 156
   cost control in, 80
   limitations of, 157
   and "play or pay" system, 168
   projected increase for, 113
   as social insurance, 155, 156
Menke, Terri, 163n
Meyer, Jack A., 164n
Michigan, single business tax in, 144
Miller, John A., 143n
Minority groups, and economic inequality, 38–39. *See also* Blacks
Misery index, 57
Moynihan, Daniel P., 173
Murnane, Richard J., 72n

Nathan, Richard, 101, 102
National Bellas Hess v. *Illinois Department of Revenue*, 139n

National Defense Education Act, 92
National health insurance, 165–66
   and medicare, 168
National income, per capita, 35–36
National Leadership Coalition for
   Health Care Reform, 163, 166
National security
   economic dimension of, 22–24
   environmental dimension of, 24–25
   military dimension of, 21–22
   in *1990s*, 27–29
   political dimension of, 25
Negative income tax (NIT), 97–98
New Deal, 87–88
New Federalism, 100, 123
   "dividing the job" compared with,
      125
   and Reagan swap proposal, 124–25
Nixon, Richard M., 55, 97–98, 100
Nuclear proliferation, 10, 21–22
Nuclear weapons production, envi-
   ronmental damage from, 64

Oil shock (*1973*), 57, 66, 146
Oil shock (*1979*), 57, 146
Osborne, David, 18–19, 181n
Ozone layer depletion, 10, 25

Peace dividend, and health cost divi-
   dend, 164
Pechman, Joseph A., 100n
Pereira, Joseph, 141n
Persian Gulf war. *See* Gulf war
Peterson, Paul, 121–22
"Play or pay" health insurance sys-
   tem, 166–67
Policy process
   faults of, 3
   improvement of, 181–82
Political discourse, 2
   and cold war secrecy, 29
   need for participation in, 3
Political parties, lack of agendas of, 2
Political system. *See* Democratic po-
   litical system
Population growth, as international
   problem, 28
Poverty
   and blacks, 49, 61
   decline of ("good news" years),
      46–49

in "disappointing" years, 42, 59–60
during Great Depression, 46–47
as international problem, 28
official definition of, 47–48
and social insurance, 90
war on, 95–98
Presidency, improved staffing for, 103
Private enterprise
and individual empowerment, 182
and pragmatism, 4
Productivity, 65–66
causes of decline, 66–68
in "disappointing" years, 59, 66–68
and "dividing the job" scenario, 118
and education reform, 68–69, 72, 74
in "eighties continued" scenario, 114
during "good news" years, 45
and international role, 11
need to increase, 6, 81
prescriptions for increasing, 68–70
and restructuring of companies, 180
and social security claims, 174
as state function, 8, 17, 118
Public capital, and economic sustainability, 39–40
Public investment
and "back to the sixties" scenario, 115
during "disappointing years," 63–64

Quality of life, deterioration of, 2, 36

Rabe, Barry G., 121n
Rafuse, Robert W., Jr., 134n
R&D (research and development)
need to increase, 81
and productivity drop (1970s), 67
and productivity improvement, 70
Reagan, Ronald, and Reagan administration, 70, 75, 101–02, 123–25
Reapportionment, 105–06
states' neglect of, 94
Recession
of 1974–75, 57, 59, 61

of 1980–82, 58, 61, 129–30
of 1990, 70, 133
Research and development. See R&D
Retail sales tax. See Sales tax, common shared state
Revenue sharing, 99–100, 125
poorer states favored in, 136
and Reagan revolution, 102
and Reagan swap proposal, 125
reverse, 143
special, 123
and states' skepticism, 148
Reynolds v. Sims, 105
Roosevelt, Franklin D., 47, 87
Rosenthal, Alan, 105n

Sabato, Larry, 104n
"Safety net," vs. social insurance, 155
Sala-i-Martin, Xavier, 135n
Sales tax, common shared state, 17–18, 127, 142–43
Sanford, Terry, 93, 94n
Saving, private and public
collapse of (1980s), 74–78
during "disappointing" years, 61–63
as federal function, 13
during "good news" years, 53–55
need to increase, 6, 7, 172, 179
policies for increasing, 77
and social security surpluses, 77–78, 172–73
Schultze, Charles L., 44n
Service industries, productivity during "disappointing years," 59
Shannon, John, 84n, 107n
Sharing of economic goods. See Distribution of income
Silow-Carroll, Sharon, 164n
Single-parent families, 60, 61
Single-payer system of health care, 163–64, 165–66
Small, Kenneth A., 40n, 70n, 146n
Smoot-Hawley Tariff Act (1930), 88
Social insurance, 88–89, 154–56
as federal function, 153
and health insurance reform, 156–68
social security, 88–89, 168–76 (see also Social security)
See also Entitlement programs

Social security, 88–89, 168–70
  benefit levels under, 170
  benefit reductions under, 173–76
  and "disappointing years," 59
  and federal budget deficit, 78, 172, 173
  as federal success, 12
  in "good news" years, 50
  indexing of benefits, 59, 170
  and national saving, 13, 172–73
  projections for, 111–13, 171
  reserves in, 77–78, 170–72
  retirement age increase for, 175
Soviet Union, and cold war, 26–27
Special revenue sharing, 123
Stagflation, 57
Standard of living
  during "disappointing years," 58–59
  in "eighties continued" scenario, 114
  expectation of improvement in, 35–38
  and fading of American dream, 1–2, 177
  during "good news" years, 43–45
  and health care cost control, 158, 164
  and productivity growth, 66
  protectionism as reducing, 27
State-federal relationship. *See* Federalism; Federalism, types of; Historical evolution of federalism
State government
  common shared taxes for, 8, 17–18, 118, 127, 142–52, 180 (*see also* Common shared state taxes)
  dissatisfaction with (*1930s-60s*), 9, 92–94
  in "dividing the job" scenario, 118–19
  governors, 93, 102–05
  and industrial policy, 120–21
  and interstate activities, 12
  legislatures, 93, 105–06
  and productivity agenda, 8, 17, 118
  reforms in, 102–07
  See also "Dividing the job" scenario
State and local government
  under dual federalism, 85
  fiscal crisis of, 2, 14–15

  proper functions for, 81, 179
  and Reagan cuts, 102
  services reserved to, 91
  social problems facing, 130–31
State revenue increase, 126–27
  through common shared taxes, 127, 142–52
  and fiscal stress, 129–33
  and German approach, 150–51
  and go-it-alone tax initiatives, 139–42
  and interstate competition, 137–39
  and sources of revenue, 127–29
  and unequal resources, 133–37
State taxes. *See* Taxes, state
Steuerle, C. Eugene, 159n
Stockman, David, 101
Strauss, Robert P., 145n
Suburbanization
  and "disappointing" years, 63
  in "good news" years, 49–50, 56
Sullivan, Sean, 164n
Supplementary security income program (SSI), 60, 98
  cost-of-living indexing for, 71
Supply-side economics, 4–5, 120
Sustainability, of economic growth, 39–41
Swap proposal (Reagan), 123–25

Tax credits, federal, 149–50
Taxes, federal
  in "back to the sixties" scenario, 115–16
  during "disappointing years," 71
  under dual federalism, 85
  in German federal system, 18, 150–51
  in "good news" period, 51–52
  and growth of federal institutions, 91
  and health insurance, 117, 159
  income tax initiated, 85
  and inflation, 107
  multiple systems of, 136
  need to increase, 13–15, 81, 117
  and negative income tax, 97–98
  in *1960–90*, 75, 76
  as politically risky, 113
  in Reagan swap proposal, 124
  social insurance, 16, 89

on social security benefits, 169,
175–76
social security payroll, 16, 71, 107,
173
value-added, 144–45, 151, 168n
and voter dissatisfaction, 16
Taxes, state
and catalog sales, 139
common shared, 8, 17–18, 118,
127, 142–52, 180 (*see also* Common shared state taxes)
Florida service tax, 139–41
increases in, 16, 71
interstate competition over, 137–39
and interstate inequalities, 133–35
Massachusetts service tax, 141–42
and multistate businesses, 136–37,
138, 145
need to increase, 15, 180
in *1980*s, 130
and 1990–92 recession, 133
in Reagan swap proposal, 124
reforms of, 106–07
sources of, 127–28
voter support, 16
See also State revenue increase
Tax pyramiding, 140
Technology, and health care costs,
80, 159
Trade. *See* International trade, U.S.
Training
improvement of, 72–74
and productivity, 68–69
See also Education
Transportation systems
in "good news" years, 50
improvements needed in, 69–70
interstate highway system, 50,
135–36
See also Infrastructure
Trippett, Frank, 93

Unemployment
among black males, 60
during "disappointing" years,
57–58
during Great Depression, 46–47,
87
Unemployment insurance, 89
United Nations, 26

Value-added tax (VAT), 118–19, 143
common shared state, 17–18,
118–19, 143–45
German, 151
for health insurance, 168n
Van Horn, Carl E., 103n, 105n
Vietnam War, 57

War on poverty, 95–98
Watergate scandals, 57
Weapons proliferation, 21–22
Weld, William, 142
Welfare benefits, decline in, 71
Welfare programs, 88, 89–90
under "dividing the job" scenario,
119
growth of, 98
vs. guaranteed income, 97
See also Entitlement programs
Williams, Robin M., Jr., 49n
Winston, Clifford, 40n, 70n, 146n
Women, during "disappointing"
years, 58, 61, 67
Wong, Kenneth K., 121n
World Bank, 26
World War II
economy revived by, 87
and federal income tax rates, 91
and "good news" years, 43
and saving, 53–54

Yankelovich, Daniel, 16n, 181n